Dedicated to:

My children -
Christopher, Andrea, Geoffrey,
Charlotte and Michael

Acknowledgements

To the many friends and people I thought were not friends at the time, but who were mirroring different aspects of me, and through their hard words or deeds inspired me to achieve and rise to greater heights and helped me to learn that I had to 'Pick myself up, dust myself off and start all over again'! Suffering enables us to understand the problems of others and gives us more compassion, love and tolerance.

If my early life had been too easy I wouldn't have striven to work and achieve my goals. I now have a wonderful family and I love my work, scuba diving, skiing and fun. I have my own businesses, financial abundance, fitness and health, five lovely children and loving friends; I feel very fulfilled and proud of my achievements. I feel more aligned with the energy flow of the universe, feeling the flow of energy of enjoyment, creativity, money, appreciation and the excitement of challenge. I want you to have it all as well. You create it all so why not create a happy and prosperous life for yourself.

Contents

'Give of your love for when you give love you receive love tenfold more

Give of your belongings for when you give you make way for more

Give of yourself. To some your smile is worth a million dollars.

Love all, spread your love, spread your joy, keep your peace within. Quietly centred you will radiate and resonate to all a beacon of light

Go forth - go forth and light up the lives of all - for all are worthy -

Let your laughter and joy spread through the universe

You are love, joy and peace

Let peace remain in your spirit dear one

Sprinkle your magic to all'
Carmel Greenwood

Preface

This book is like a potluck dinner. The hostess has lovingly prepared and set the table but if no one brings any food there is nothing to eat.

If you do not have anything at stake this book will be of no value to you. Only if you are at a time in your life when you need and want to create change will you receive benefit.

Many people asked me to write this book when they saw tremendous change in me and the creation of my new life. I have learnt a great deal in writing it and trust you will gain as much from reading it.

Carmel Greenwood

Introduction

You cannot change or do anything unless you can first visualize yourself being what you want to be and see yourself in a loving, successful, prosperous environment, or doing what you want to do.

You can go to course after course and read book after book - that's all some people do – but unless you are honest with yourself and are committed and can see yourself as changing and visualize a different self image, you will stay as you are. It takes discipline to take the time to meditate and visualize, but once you believe and decide to do it, you can, and will. When you are willing to let go, clear your mind and reprogram your conscious mind; it will happen. The choice is yours.

Have you ever wondered why some people seem to 'have it all'? They are happy, abundant, healthy and peaceful and have joy and love in their lives. They are just lucky, you might say. But that's not true. People make their own luck and are as happy, wealthy and wise as they make up their minds to be. You create your own reality and the life you are living now was created by you and by your thoughts. If you don't like the way you are living now, you can change it. You can change your thought patterns to surround yourself with new energy and choose a different reality. There are no accidents – you create your own reality by your thoughts, your direction of energy, your belief structure and your perception of how life should be. If you don't expect it and it isn't in your belief structure, it won't happen. Everyone, regardless of position, circumstances, status or health, is in control of their own experience. If you are in poor health, you can remedy it; if your personal relationships are unsatisfactory, you can change them for the better; if you are in poverty, you can find yourself surrounded by abundance...

Many people have asked me how I can accomplish the many things I do and still remain sane and enjoy life to the full. I have five children, am a successful author and speaker, I travel and enjoy scuba diving and skiing. The answer is I have created my life now the way I want it to be.

Twenty years ago, however, my life was very different. I was a complete 'victim', drifting along and accepting everything that came upon me. I felt trapped and miserable until I met a friend. When I told him my tale of woe he laughingly told me, 'You create your own reality. If you don't like your life now, re-create it.' That is a very simple statement, isn't it? I thought at the time that my friend was crazy but realize now that you can create and do anything you want. There are no limitations. That statement finally had such an impact on me that I have re-created a happy, fulfilled and abundant life for myself. Now I want to share with you the many wonderful things I have learned and the methods I have found to be the most practical and useful.

Through using creative imagery and visualization in alpha meditation I changed myself and my thoughts and I have made tapes to guide you, to relax, clarify and slow down your mind, release stress and create your life the way you want it to be. This book and my tapes are my gift to you in love. May they give you prosperity, joy, laughter, love, peace and health. Why not create a good world for yourself. Prosperity is not just for the few who were born under a lucky star or who were born to a wealthy family. It is for everyone. But why don't we all have it? If things are not as you wish now, it is because of the way you are thinking. It does not just 'happen' to you, you see. You can make it happen.

Chapter 1

Belief structures and perception

Why are all people different and why don't we all think the same way? Life would be so much easier if everyone thought the same way and had the same expectations. Why don't they? It is all in our belief structures and the feelings we have about ourselves and the way the world works.

How are belief structures and perceptions of the world formed? We usually have a set of limiting, negative beliefs about ourselves and how the universe works. The problem with these beliefs is that they are based on our own perceptions and false conclusions that we received from our parents, teachers and society around us. We were told things like 'money is the root of all evil', 'you'll never learn', 'you are clumsy', 'you're in the way', 'you'll never get anywhere', 'don't do that, you'll hurt yourself, you'll fall', 'you'll be sorry', etc. etc. This is all recorded in our conscious and sub-conscious minds and as adults when we try to achieve anything, the recording of negative thoughts replays and reminds us why we can't achieve that goal or objective. Ultimately, these beliefs are not true, but because we are creators of our own experience of reality, they seem to us to be true because we believe in them. We see evidence of them reflected in the world and we remain loyal to our parents at all costs in having full faith that the way they operated in the world was 100 percent correct.

The beliefs that result in self-image centre around the illusion of limitation, guilt, fear, rejection, sacrifice and pain and the ideas that life is a struggle, you mustn't enjoy yourself, or that money is evil. You may think the world is a hostile place where you are a victim of forces outside over which you have no control, but it isn't.

My personal experiences and what they taught me

This was really made clear to me when I spent two months in hospital observing the welcome or rejection that babies received before and after they were born. At 31 weeks pregnant, I had placenta previa when I was having my fifth baby, Michael, and had to be rushed to hospital because I was haemorrhaging badly. The bleeding wouldn't stop and after six hours my doctor had to transfer me to a hospital in Hong Kong where they had facilities for premature babies. They thought they would have to deliver Michael that night and his chances for survival at 31 weeks weren't good. I had to stop the bleeding. I meditated and spoke to Michael and told him it wasn't time to come yet. The bleeding finally stopped but the doctors told me I had to stay in hospital until he was born.

I am a very active person and besides having a business to run and my family to care for, the thought of two months in hospital made me feel sorry for myself and depressed. That lasted for a few hours until I realized that I had created this situation for a reason. I used the time to meditate and read, and for the first time in my life to allow myself to take time off. I had always run around doing things to keep myself busy and now I was forced to get in touch with my inner self, learn humility and resolve some personal issues.

I was in a public ward for all the special maternity cases that needed special care and attention. I was the only European in a Chinese-speaking ward and it was extremely noisy most of the time. There were women in labour, babies crying and the usual activity of a busy hospital; the surroundings were grim and depressing but the staff were completely dedicated and they were on duty for long hours with very little sleep.

To leave the surroundings I meditated a lot. I went anywhere I wanted to go with alpha meditation and visualization; I went skiing in Switzerland, scuba diving in the South Pacific, and I spent time with my family seeing the good times and visualizing my new baby – how strong and healthy he would be. I talked to him all the time. I imagined taking my new baby home to my loving family. I didn't dwell on bad thoughts, although the negativity kept creeping in. Indeed, I tried to concentrate on positive thoughts and use my time constructively.

Our beliefs affect our lives

It was very interesting in the ward to see the casualties come in and watch how each woman handled herself. Some were brave and in charge and others completely out of control. Although the nurses were tolerant and the doctors superb, the patients were screaming at the doctors and staff because of their discomfort. They did not consider for a moment that the doctor hadn't had any sleep for the past 14 hours and had many other patients to attend to. They wanted full attention just for themselves and demanded it. They created their own reality of disharmony and difficulty in delivering their baby – and blamed everyone for their discomfort. Most had difficult deliveries and

I am sure the babies already knew and accepted from their own birth that 'life is a struggle'. They had already formed their beliefs. When they were finally born, their mothers didn't want to hold them and felt resentment towards them. 'This horrible baby gave me all this pain, I hate it.' The baby felt rejected, unloved: 'What a hostile world this is, I cry and cry and nobody cares,' and forms the belief, 'If I haven't had love how can I give love?' The mothers who worked with their babies, held, accepted and loved them immediately, had easier deliveries and their babies formed a belief structure that their world was a nice, loving place to be in. 'I feel loved and wanted, I can go into the world and give love.'

The unity surrounds you – accept it

Even before birth, the outer environment influences the developing foetus, especially the consciousness and environment of the parents. The environment and circumstances in which a person is being born influences the mental state of the foetus. Children's potentials can be suppressed or enhanced by parental words, attitudes and actions. For instance, if parents want their baby to become a doctor or dentist when the baby came to this world to be a teacher or artist, the child may have to work through extra guilt, anxiety or anger in order to actualize his or her goals.

I had delivered my four other babies completely naturally and was disappointed that I had to have a Caesarean section delivery. But I had managed to keep Michael from being born until 37 weeks and he was perfectly healthy and didn't need an incubator at all. He was just how I had imagined him – a beautiful and healthy, joyful and happy baby.

Forming my belief structure

On a subconscious level we all repeat what we saw and heard our parents doing. When they get married, girls strangely seem to turn into their mothers (many men complain). This isn't really so strange – girls are acting out their own reality of how they think the world operates and the man they marry, in their belief system, should be the way their father was. That is why there can be problems in marriage and relationships, when each partner has a different set of belief structures and their expectations of each other may be quite different, especially if they are not the same nationality and had a completely different way of growing up.

I married my first husband in 1968 after I had known him for about six months. We were living in Hong Kong, an exciting and dynamic place. He was working in a very stressful job, on call 24 hours a day and was a man's man. He was full of charm and fun, but he loved to drink and spent most of his time drinking at his favourite club. Women at that time were not even allowed into the bar. He was ten years older than I was (as my father had been to my mother). I worked at the airport, came home and prepared dinner and waited for my husband to come home. He rarely did, since he was often out drinking with his friends. I sat at home and wondered what was wrong with me and thought it was my fault that he preferred to stay out so much.

But subconsciously I was re-creating the life my mother had. That was my belief structure of how life worked. I used to sit with my mother as a child and she would be crying and wondering why my father constantly came home late. She blamed herself and thought it was her fault.

I thought that maybe if my first husband and I had a family he would come home more. I had two lovely children, but nothing changed. After I had my first son, I went back to work after two month's maternity leave. We needed the money and I was the devoted wife and tried to do everything perfectly – work and look after my baby. My husband thought I had become boring. I suppose I was. I was up feeding my son, working all day and didn't have time for fun. Life was supposed to be a struggle, you had to be the martyr and men were selfish. That was my perception of how the world worked. I had turned into my mother and married the man who would repeat what my father had done to prove my belief. My husband didn't like the responsibility of a wife and family. I accepted my 'lot' but was very lonely and cried frequently, just as I had seen my mother do when I was a child. I thought the same things she had repeated many times – 'all men are selfish' – and I had proved it, hadn't I? Poor little me, sitting at home with two babies, taking all the responsibility and no one to care for me. I felt unloved and wasn't enjoying my life very much. I had subconsciously drawn to me the man who would best play out my own reality and belief structure of how my world worked. I had proved myself right.

I was a real victim. I used to get out of bed and say: 'I wonder what is going to happen to me today? What a life, everything awful happens to me! It's just not fair! I'm married to an alcoholic and never know what he is going to do next! I don't have any money. I can't leave; with children to support I would never survive. If I could earn lots of money then I would be OK, but I'm stupid, how could I ever earn enough money? I'll never get anywhere. Better stay here, at least I'm safe, at least I have a roof over my head!'

I heard my mother's voice: 'You have made your own bed my girl – you'd better lie in it!' 'Don't come home to me with two kids!' 'I told you so – all men are selfish!'

'It's not fair,' I whined.

'Whoever said life was fair,' she said, 'It's a struggle!'

Sound familiar? That was my 'belief' of how the world worked. A great attitude. I wonder why I wasn't doing too well?

Things got worse and he was drinking more. One day the doorbell rang at 4am. He had been drinking and had fallen asleep at the wheel of the car and crashed into the back of a bus. He had crashed our new car and went out through the wind-

screen and landed on the road. I went to visit him at the hospital
and thought, why have I got myself into this situation? I had
stopped working for a brief period, had no money, my husband
was nearly dead and I had babies to support. He recovered and
six months later crashed another car, which he had borrowed.

I was depressed, desperate and unhappy. I had
tried to be a devoted, hardworking wife. But
life didn't have anything for me. I felt
unloved, resentful and full of anger at him
and my life. He loved me as best as he
knew how, but when I look back at myself
now, I was exactly like my mother – the
martyr. I was there to serve my family and I
felt my life was over. What had happened to the
child in me? It was overtaken by responsibility. I was
unbalanced. I had over-identified with my nurturing, giving side
and devoted myself exclusively to family. I became overly critical
and judgmental. I thought I had failed at my marriage and I was
a failure. I had proved my belief that I was not good enough,
didn't measure up and wasn't loveable!

The power is with you – use it. The wisdom is in you – employ it

I had to do something positive. I read Norman Vincent
Peale's book *The Power of Positive Thinking*, which at that time
was helpful. However, most books on positive thinking alone,
while beneficial, usually do not take into account the habitual
nature of negative feelings, aggressions or repressions. They are
merely swept under the carpet. They tell you to be positive, com-
passionate, optimistic and strong, filled with joy and enthusiasm,
without telling you what to do to get out of the predicament you
may be in, and without understanding the vicious circle that
seems to trap you. These books do not explain how thoughts and
emotions cause reality and do not take into consideration all the
aspects of the self and how each person finds their own way of
adapting to their own personal circumstances.

Then I met my friend who after I had told him my 'victim'

story told me, 'You create your own reality.' I finally 'got it'. It took some time, but after meditating and talking to him at length it made sense. I understood that I was responsible for what was happening to me and whatever my circumstances were at birth and whatever poverty, sickness or bad relationship I found myself in now, things could be changed for the better. I realized that I was not powerless to change anything in my life, and with determination and effort I could change and re-create whatever circumstance I found myself in to what I wanted. If I did not like my experience, I could change my conscious thoughts and expectations and change the messages I was sending through my thoughts to my own body and to friends and colleagues. Each thought has a result. If I changed my thoughts, I changed my reality. We often blame others – parents, spouse or our background – for our difficulties, but no one forces us to think in a particular manner. We may believe that pessimism is more realistic than optimism, that sorrow or being a martyr a sign of deep spiritualism and to suffer is saintly. Nothing could be further from the truth.

Love is the answer – give it

I met an aristocratic Lord in Europe and we were talking about beliefs and I said I had come from the edge of the Nullabor Plain in the outback of Australia and now came to own this lovely home. He said pensively, 'My father always told me I would end up in a semi-detached house and that is where I am now.' I smiled sweetly and said, 'Well, that was your problem, you believed him!' 'My father worked in a gold mine and did not give me any money but I knew I could manifest anything I really wanted. You started out with a whole castle and through your underlying belief, circumstances happened that you had to sell the castle and move into several smaller houses until you reached your destination of your father's programming and your belief that all you deserved was a semi-detached house.

'How did this come about? This reversal of fortunes is not where you came from and where you went to school. It is how you think and what limitations you place on yourself that will manifest for you.'

In a few words ■ ■ ■ ■ ■ ■ ■ ■ ■ ■ ■ ■ ■

Man has been given a conscious mind to form his own creations. Only when you refuse to take responsibility do you seem to be at the mercy of events over which it appears you have no control.

We all have problems. The only people without problems are six feet under, in the cemetery! We could be problem free and join them, but it is not the answer. Problems are for growth.

When your mind is troubled, use what energy you have for centring and the problems will solve themselves. Do not solicit external crutches. In the essence of your being begin your search for peace in the place you find peace, for there is an environment you have experienced that is more compatible with your energy than any other.
Listen in silence and through the sound of silence, your heart will speak to you with a voice you cannot ignore.

Make your decisions and stand by them, for in commitment there is strength. Walk in freedom without looking behind you, without guilt – the most foolish of emotions. Your only problems are those you choose to accept.

■ ■

Chapter 2

You create your own reality

Think how your lifestyle would change today if you truly believed you were a great and glorious person with something valuable to contribute. How would you live and dress? What would be different about you? Everything you say, do and have expresses your beliefs. An image of success requires radical change to your basic self-image that is hard to handle. If success should come before the self-image is ready for it, you will do whatever is necessary to put the brakes on and stop it. When you experience true prosperity you are accepted by the world as worthy. This is very hard to take before you have accepted your own worthiness. If you like yourself and you think you are a nice person, nice things will happen to you. If you love yourself and have self-worth then nothing in this world can touch you.

Fear of success is a barrier to your development when it keeps you from developing your full potential. Those who dare risk and achieve are painful reminders of what you are not doing. To avoid this pain you condemn with envy and jealousy, or you admire with awe. Both responses separate you from others. Only when you are able to truly appreciate and enjoy the success of others are you setting up the right mental attitude to be successful yourself. Fear of failure and success stems from lack of self-acceptance. You must realize you are in control and you have only you to please – you decide the goal and pace.

Some people, mostly women, try to compensate for a low self-image by being the best at everything: a super person at home, job and relationships. This covers up deeper feelings that they must always prove themselves to someone. It comes from not feeling 'good enough'. For whom? Ourselves, of course. Or we can devise a plot that proves we are no good by overspending, overeating, getting drunk or playing the martyr. For example, by staying with an alcoholic mate who has no intention of changing, we may be expressing a need to be put down or feel like the healthy one in a relationship or perform the miracle of changing another. Sometimes our entire focus is on someone or something other than ourselves. We spend years worrying about, reacting to and trying to control others. With all this energy

in a few words ■ ■ ■ ■ ■ ■ ■ ■ ■ ■ ■ ■ ■ ■ ■

Richard Bach said, 'Argue for your limitations and they are yours.' Some people have a life-theme of believing that they can't have what they want in life and they often don't get it. They always prove themselves right. Whatever you believe you get!

If you believe and say you never have enough money, you will be poor; if you believe you have abundance, you will. If you believe you are powerless, you will be. Whatever you believe about yourself and the world, you will create it.

■ ■

directed at others, our own is depleted, until we don't even know what we are thinking and feeling. Our focus is outside of ourselves. We choose men who reject us and prove that all men are unworthy and prove that we are unlovable.

We repeat this game until we finally, if ever, understand that we, and only we, create our own reality. But you don't have to be a victim, you can call the shots and act, not be acted on. Act first instead of re-acting to situations.

Overcoming victimization

You either take responsibility for your life or you feel victimized by the world. Your choice to play the victim or to take responsibility will determine whose power grows – yours or someone else's. If you choose responsibility, you have the power to do something about the situation. For example, if you take responsibility for your husband/wife leaving you when you didn't want him/her to, you are free to look at the ways you helped set up the relationship so he/she would want to leave. You can then learn from the experience and learn what you don't want to do next time.

Being a victim takes a tremendous amount of energy. Wallowing in self pity, feeling bad, hurt, angry, insecure, unattractive, guilty, resentful and blaming others for your feelings of unworthiness holds you back from accepting yourself as the confident, beautiful, creative, passionate, spontaneous, loving person you truly are.

The payoffs you get from being a victim are sympathy, attention, people help you, and you can prove yourself right that you are not loveable and acceptable. You can manipulate and self-sabotage relationships to prove to yourself that you are a bad person. You feel incomplete and your self-esteem is so low that you want others to constantly fill you up, to approve and love you. You give but want approval and love from others in return so badly that it is giving with hooks, conditional love.

It never works. When you can surrender and know that you are the source and can fill your own cup, you do not have to struggle any more, you are free and know that everything will come to you. You do not have to be a victim and manipulate and control to get what you want, you can take responsibility for yourself and ask for what you want in an honest, direct way and get it.

Victims are like cows, mooing for approval and love, accepting anything that comes along, that is dished out. Not sticking up for themselves and never feeling adequate, satisfied and good about themselves, 'the moo-cows' reach out for encouragement and receive rejection. Feeling lonely and after giving and giving, the supply seems to dry up. The victim numbs him or herself and cannot give any more. Tired from the enormous burden, the victim becomes hostile and angry but keeps 'helping' and resenting.

Having low self-worth and feeling unlovable, you do not feel good about yourself so you settle for feeling needed and compelled to do things for others to prove how good you are, constantly trying to gain self-worth and power. But these feelings are temporary and momentarily distract you from the pain of being who you are. You learn to cope, to survive by picking up and assuming other people's responsibilities. You believe you cannot be selfish, must be kind and help people, never hurt other people's feelings because you 'make them feel', must not mention your personal wants and needs because it is not polite and you must never say no.

You may have been taught to be responsible for other people, but not responsible for yourself; that good, desirable mothers/fathers, wives/husbands are caretakers, responsible for every family member. But caretaking and rescuing is self-destructive and can breed anger, frustration and confusion. The people you constantly help either are or become helpless, angry and manipulating victims.

It is not good to take care of people who take advantage of you to avoid responsibility. It hurts them and you. Caretaking people is pleasing and martyrdom and not taking care of yourself. Co-dependents rescue, then they persecute, then they feel victimized. It is a pattern that is repeated with family, friends and those around. You fix, make better, solve, take care of people's responsibilities for them and then get angry with them for what you have done, then you feel sorry for yourself. Enabling is a destructive way of helping because it enables the person not to take responsibility for their life. By continuously helping my alcoholic mate, preventing him from suffering consequences, I helped him to continue drinking.

You rescue when you take responsibility for another person's thoughts, decisions, behaviour, growth, problems, feelings or destiny. You also rescue when you say yes when you mean no; doing what you do not really want to do; speaking for another person; solving other people's problems for them; fixing people's feelings; suffering people's consequences for them; continuously giving more than you receive, and not asking for what you need, want and desire.

When you caretake or rescue you feel pity, guilt, anxiety, fear, resentment, saintliness, extreme responsibility and feel needed temporarily. You rescue 'victims' then feel resentful and angry with the person you have 'helped'. You did something you did not want to do and ignored your own needs and wants. The poor victim is not grateful and appreciative of your sacrifice and you resent and blame that person and feel angry with him or her. You feel hurt, helpless and sorry. You have been used and unappreciated and trampled on. You try so hard to help people and this is what you get back! You turn into the victim. It is a vicious cycle.

It is all too easy to allow oneself to be victimized as a child. Many of us were true victims of someone's abuse, neglect, alcoholism and abandonment and were helpless to solve or protect ourselves. The result is hurt and a continuation of the patterns well into adulthood until we realize what we are doing: taking responsibility for everybody and anybody except ourselves. Imagine two people-pleasers in a relationship, which they would really like to end but neither will take the responsibility for ending it. They would rather destroy each other and themselves before wanting to be the guilty one to finish it.

I think I wanted my ex-husband to be the guilty one, and by him attempting to strangle me, I was the innocent, saintly one who was victimized and could leave as an innocent victim. I was not the guilty one who had ended the relationship. It was not my fault, I was the 'goodie!'

You tell yourself you are unworthy, so you do not have to take responsibility for yourself completely; you are a bad mother or father, so you do not have to live up to your responsibilities; you are not honest with yourself, so you do not have to commit and be honest; you do not get love, so you do not have to give it. Besides taking a tremendous amount of energy, what is missing in your life is freedom to be what and who you really are, the courage to say what you want, need and feel.

> Instead of being a sad victim with fears and tears, choose love, laughter, bliss and freedom

You can decide to let go of the victim and realize that you matter and count, you are important, and take the responsibility to ask for love, encouragement and support. Be vulnerable and know that you do not always have to be the strong person who looks after everyone else but not yourself. You can let go of your old hurts, blame and resentment and be honest with yourself and ask for love and acceptance from those you love.

Most of us have survived all our lives by saying what others want us to say, and doing what others want us to do. But when you can be honest with yourself, stand by your convictions and know that it is okay if some people do not like you for saying what they do not want to hear, you escape victimization. Ultimately, it is serving them to tell the truth of how you feel about them, not holding back but speaking the truth of what you feel at the time. Live your life with integrity, open up and share what you feel, give love and ask for love in return. Take responsibility for your life and live it the way you want to create it. Take a stand and make a difference in the world, create love and abundance and choose to live with total responsibility for your own happiness. Let others be responsible for themselves and live fully, spontaneously, with vitality and enthusiasm. Commit to humanity with honest and direct communication and stand up for what you believe.

In a few words ■ ■ ■ ■ ■ ■ ■ ■ ■ ■ ■ ■ ■ ■

When you can let go of the victim, you let go of your armour and reveal the hurt person you are, you will be free to live your life in an honest way, and give up the struggle, trying to protect yourself from hurt, pretending to be strong and tough.

Instead of feeling trapped inside your steel armour, you can allow yourself to be vulnerable and break your way out and show and share what a beautiful, loveable person you really are. Most of us have flaws and peculiar habits, but when you can accept yourself the way you are, life becomes a creative adventure where you can be confident, happy, powerful and in charge.

Refuse to rescue and refuse to let people rescue you. Take responsibility for yourself and let others do the same. Whether you change your behaviour, your mind, your circumstances or attitudes, the kindest thing you can do is to remove the victim – yourself.

I am not saying do not give love, kindness, compassion and true helping to situations that genuinely need and want your help, only stop the rescuing or caretaking.

■ ■

Don't blame others

Responsibility can be rejected because it is confused with blame. If I am responsible then I am to blame, or if I take responsibility, the other person gets off free without guilt. Blame is only a judgement – anger at yourself for feeling stuck. If you are blaming others – parents, spouse, friends – it is time to let go of these negative, poisonous feelings for your own benefit and get on with life. Give up being a victim. No one has power over you unless you give it to him or her. If there are things in your life you don't like, don't moan and groan, change them.

Parents are usually blamed for most of our faults – why we aren't the most successful, generous, loveable people imaginable. If it wasn't for 'them' I would be the most perfect, wonderful person alive! We feel ruined for life by what our parents did or didn't do in bringing us up. 'If only they had done this, or sent me to that school, or done that,' we moan, 'I would be different now.' There is such a thing as parent abuse. Whether parents are to blame or not is irrelevant. But it is time to get on with your life now! Forget about all the garbage that happened before. Throw it away and don't judge, only learn from your experiences and do this without blaming yourself, your parents, ex-husband/wife, ex-boyfriend/girlfriend, or whoever you have a hate or resentment towards.

You gain in power and energy each time you can identify the choices you made in attitude and behaviour and the benefits and strength you received by creating your formative life. We all carry so much excess baggage around with us with all our old hates, resentments, worry and negative thinking. It is very heavy, but when you decide to let it go you feel much lighter and have much more energy.

My parents weren't in a position to give me more than I had. Their circumstances and own upbringing related and dictated as to how I was brought up. From their limited resources they did the best they could in the circumstances and in the only way they knew how. It may not have been right, but from their resources and past experiences and perceptions of how the world worked it was the right way for them.

It was my choice to change, disregard or use whatever my perception of life is now to bring up my own children. It may not be the correct way and parents make mistakes, they are human too, but I think every parent does the best they can in their own circumstances and environment. If a parent didn't receive love as a child himself/herself, it is very difficult for them to show and say 'I love you' to their own children unless they change their belief structure, get rid of their old conditioning and replace it with positive energy. Their programming gets replayed and replayed to the next generations and will continue to be passed on unless you change the record and re-program. Accept your parents the way they are. Try to see why they are the way they are and realize where they are coming from. Give them your unconditional love to be themselves. Don't try to change them; it must be for them to decide how they want to live their own lives. Leave them alone and start caring for yourself instead.

In   a   few   words ■■■■■■■■■■■■■■■

Let's all stop blaming and judging. People are learning entities. If you drop 'should' from your life and do what you want to do, you will feel alive and fulfilled.

■■■■■■■■■■■■■■■■■■■■■■■■■■■

Forgive yourself and others

As you learn to give more and forgive more, instead of getting and blaming, you can see why it is important to let go of condemnation, blame and guilt. In doing this, you realize that you must accept responsibility for your own freedom and happiness since you can be hurt by nothing but your own thoughts. Forgive all that have offended you – not for them, but for yourself. You do not need to wait until others deserve your forgiveness, because you are not doing it for them. By holding resentments against others, you hurt yourself more than anyone else. Forgiving is an act of giving.

After 15 years of marriage, and after my ex-husband had been drunk and physically violent, he tried to strangle me one night. I finally realized I had to leave him. I had been fooling myself into believing that I was staying 'for the sake of the children'. They had witnessed this nasty scene and I knew I had to go, even though my belief at that time was 'Marriage was for better or for worse, in sickness and in health, till death do us part.'

Just before my father died, he asked me to forgive my ex-husband. I said I never would because of all the terrible things he had done to hurt me. With all the humiliation and hurt I had suffered why should I forgive him? After my father died his message kept preying on my mind and I thought, 'Okay just for him I will do it. Here goes!' I phoned my ex-husband and said I was sorry things hadn't worked out between us but wished him well in the future. The release I had was remarkable. It was like a lead weight had been lifted from my shoulders. By forgiving and releasing him I had absolved him and myself of all guilt and had got him off my back! I could live in the 'now' and I could get on with my life and not think and go over and over again all the old garbage of who did what to whom, when! That was finished and by letting go I could start afresh and make a new life for myself. I now understand that to forgive others who have offended you is for your own benefit.

If you can write or say, 'I forgive and release you, go your own way and be happy. I forgive myself and absolve myself of all guilt, here, now and forever,' you will feel a tremendous relief. Forgiveness is the key to seeing the world differently; it is the key to happiness and offers you everything you need. It is a letting-go process that releases the past, corrects your misperceptions and stops the endless recycling of guilt.

In a few words ■ ■ ■ ■ ■ ■ ■ ■ ■ ■ ■ ■ ■

*If you truly feel you cannot forgive your parents,
friends, brothers or sisters or anyone, write it all down
on a piece of paper and frame it in a gold frame. Hang it
in the toilet – that is where all unforgiveness should go,
down the toilet. If you cannot bring yourself to flush it,
let it hang on the wall until it evaporates with all the
bad smells in there. You do not need it; it does not add
but only detracts value from your life.*

■ ■

Understanding guilt

Imagine how wonderful your life would be without guilt. We
have all suffered from feeling guilty at some stage. Guilt is
negative and destructive and is a malignancy that can kill you.
Illness is caused from the negative energy of all the stored resentments, anger and hate that you feel and have suppressed. Guilt
keeps all the past pain alive, justifies hurt, is a way of controlling
yourself and others and is a way out of avoiding the responsibility of creating your own reality. It justifies self-pity and you
can use it to try and make someone else take responsibility for
your life. When you have guilt you get stuck and can't make
decisions or choices, it fosters the victim in you. 'Poor me,' you
might say, 'I feel so guilty, and while I continue to feel guilty I
don't have to take responsibility for my own life. I will try and
get someone else to do it for me and then blame and resent him
or her when it doesn't work out.'

It is a way of being out of touch with yourself, and you
develop guilt as a tool to make it easier for relationships as a
method to control and manipulate others. It is a way of denying
openness, intimacy and keeping relationships shallow and
superficial. It is a way of avoiding self-esteem. 'If you loved me,
you would do this for me; if you loved me you wouldn't do that.'
You make the other person feel guilty so you can control them.

Guilt begins in childhood and is learnt from parents, school-teachers, churches, governments and society. Parents use it to control their children: 'If you love me, you wouldn't be naughty, I expect you to do such and such.' Insurance companies use guilt: 'If you love your family, you will insure your life for them.' Never mind if the policy doesn't keep up with inflation; you must do it so you don't have to feel guilty!

Using love to control in relationships is conditional love, which is based on limitations, qualifications and reservations, unlike unconditional love, which is based on total acceptance of oneself and others. Most of what we call love in life is conditional love, which is based on scarcity, on getting and giving to get something in return, bargaining and trading. The identifying word is 'if' – if the other person gives us what we want and changes to satisfy our needs, we feel happy; if the other person doesn't give us what we want, we feel irritated and frustrated, which leads to anger and hatred. Conditional love or love/hate relationships are built on wanting something from the other person because of a mistaken feeling of scarcity and the belief that the other person has something we lack. Fear, pain and instability are ensured because of the feelings of possessiveness, jealousy and competition that characterize conditional love.

> Take your eyes off others and look at yourself instead

Guilt is the feeling of self-condemnation when you think you have done something wrong and fear the punishment of yourself or the punishment of others. If you hold on to guilt you will attack yourself by feeling depressed or physically ill, or projecting the guilt on to someone else. When you take responsibility for your mistakes, they no longer call for guilt and punishment, but release through correction. If you feel you have offended people, you can correct your mistake by apologizing to them directly. Holding on to guilt will keep you trapped in the past by blaming others and yourself.

In a few words ■■■■■■■■■■■■■■

Guilt and negative thoughts are self-made and are a poison that we give to ourselves frequently. It is very effective in keeping you bound to your past so you cannot recognize opportunities the present offers for your release.

Complete forgiveness, starting with you, is the only release. When you accept and forgive someone or something, you are released from it and able to let go. To be truly peaceful and happy, release and forgive.

All pain is due to inability to release what needs to be free. The letting go process releases the past, corrects your misperceptions and stops the endless recycling of guilt. When you give up and release guilt you can let go of the past and get on with the future.

When you do feel negative emotions, feel sorry for yourself and lost, allow yourself to feel these emotions and know that it is okay to feel them. Don't suppress them but try to detach yourself from the situation and ask yourself why you are experiencing them, how do you feel and where are they coming from? They can be very valuable in letting you know where you are now and by detaching you will be able to get some valuable solutions to your problem.

■■■■■■■■■■■■■■■■■■■■■■■■■■■■

Releasing guilt

When you meditate, try to see the scene being played and ask yourself what your emotions are trying to tell you. They may be telling you that it is okay to feel like this, but you don't have to get stuck in them, you can change your thoughts and you can change the scene to suit you. You may feel victimized, sorry for yourself and lonely, you are clearing these emotions and moving on to something better. Take the responsibility of these emotions and analyze how you can make things better for yourself rather than trying to dump the blame on someone: parents, wife/ husband, boss or friend. Try to verbalize the feelings and come up with a solution. You don't have to stay in that situation and quite often the person who is the object of all the blame and resentment doesn't know why but can certainly feel that something is wrong. Take time for yourself and go with these feelings. Know that when your life doesn't seem to be working, it is still working perfectly.

I always tried to cover up my emotions by pretending that everything was okay and I was being silly, selfish and immature. I acted and put on a smiling mask that everything in my life was perfect. I was the best actress in town and on the surface all was well, but I was suppressing all those emotions, not allowing myself to feel them and externalizing by working long hours, socializing and laughing myself out of negativity. But I was blaming myself for having these feelings and pretending they weren't there.

I didn't know that by suppressing these emotions it was very dangerous for my health and could lead to very serious illnesses. By letting such feelings come to the surface, you can clear them. Allow yourself to feel and know that it is okay to feel and you are not a bad person for thinking bad and negative thoughts. A stiff upper lip may seem admirable, but covering up old hurts and resentments as if nothing had happened is very dangerous for the body. Big girls and boys should cry to release emotions. It is healthy. Do whatever you feel like doing alone; cry, laugh, beat your pillow and stamp your feet, or whatever feels right. By being true to yourself and your feelings you keep your balance and are centred. You don't have to take the world on your shoulders and be brave all the time. You can't save the world, but you can save yourself.

You don't have to prove your existence to anyone. Don't try to measure up to anyone else's beliefs of what is perfect. They have their own ideals and may be coming from conditional and controlling love. You are strong, just measure up to yourself and your ideals. Don't let anyone else control you. Allow yourself to have freedom, joy and happiness. Recognize your qualities and don't try to hide or hamper your growth. It is okay to wallow in self-pity and feel sorry for yourself. Recognize what you are doing and where these feelings come from. Deep breathing is also a very valuable tool to use to release negative emotions.

In a few words ■■■■■■■■■■■■■

Say goodbye to guilt, depression and despair. Place your hand in front of your head, wave goodbye to your mind, and feel from your heart.

■■■■■■■■■■■■■■■■■■■■■■■■■

Facing emotions

Because I had always suppressed my emotions and didn't allow myself to feel and had kept my anger, resentments and guilt inside, I had a series of deep-tissue massages to unblock my emotional tensions. If you suppress emotions, they get lodged in the body. They have to because they have nowhere else to go, so the body gets blocked, continuously fighting with the stresses of day-to-day living. By clearing all the energy pathways, the muscle knots and tensions areas, the body becomes clear. You become more flexible and have a lot more energy. Basically you are getting the circulation moving through your body. In getting rid of pain, it is very effective. When I first received a massage, my face was paralyzed and my hands were stiff. Amanda Edwards, the deep-tissue expert, said that was because of all the times I had suppressed and held back and hadn't said what I felt. All the emotions I hadn't expressed, especially during my childhood and my divorce, were coming out now. If I had not released them I would have some disease with my body, later in life.

You can get stuck in emotions and feel so trapped you do not know how to escape. Sadness can turn into depression and seem to last forever. Anger turns to resentment and bitterness. But repressing and denying your feelings by withdrawing and becoming unemotional is unhealthy and self-destructive and can lead to headaches, stomach problems and many illnesses. Feelings are emotional energy, and when you repress them you block your energy, which causes you to overeat or undereat or turn to compulsive spending, drugs and alcohol. When you repress your feelings and withdraw, you lose your positive feelings and ability to feel, you become numb and shut down your deep needs to love and be loved. You feel separate and lose the ability to feel intimate and enjoy the good things in life. Dealing with your feelings enables you to move out of the depths of depression, acknowledge the feeling and then move on. It is okay and essential to feel so you do not block that energy, but allow it to pass through your body. Feelings tell you about yourself and when you deal with them honestly may indicate that you need to change. Sharing feelings helps to get a better perspective and creates intimacy and closeness with another person. By being vulnerable and accepted by someone else for being who you are helps you to accept yourself.

Detachment

Until I learnt how to detach from the worry and agony of involvement of people and situations, I found it hard to solve my own problems, live my own life and feel my own feelings. My energy was scattered into solving, controlling and living the lives of others around me and reacting to their problems. I always felt responsible for the behaviour of my ex-husband and lived in fear of him making a fool of himself. I stopped inviting friends home as I never knew what to expect or how he would behave, whether he would be rude or polite. It is natural to want to protect and help the people who are close to us and react to their problems, but I had become my ex-husband's caretaker, rescuer and enabler, taking responsibility for his life as well as mine.

I had to learn that I did not have to do this. I could detach and release from taking on the responsibility of another person's life; worrying did not help and would not solve his problems for him. I had to let go and allow life to happen instead of forcing or trying to control him or it. By detaching I faced the reality of what was actually happening instead of pretending that it was not. He was physically violent and instead of denying it I faced the truth. By detaching I prevented myself from going insane. I stopped being a victim and martyr and learnt to take care of myself. It was my choice to re-create my own situation, move through my fear, agony and guilt, to let go and start to live my own life. I had had years of worrying, feeling depressed and responsible and fearing my failure in marriage, when he was destroying himself, my children and me. Survival for my children and me could only be through detachment. We could go down with the sinking ship or detach, survive and make a new life for ourselves. I gave up trying to save him and worked on saving my family and myself and raising my self-esteem. It took a while but with meditation, visualization and working on releasing my suppressed emotions, I eventually married a new man who is so secure and responsible for himself that he encourages me to be successful and grow.

Detach, let go, be responsible. Live your own life and let others live theirs

I was a constant threat to my first husband's insecurities and was criticized and made to feel inadequate all the time. By detaching I could see and think more clearly and not be so involved in the tangle of emotions, worry and grief. I stopped making excuses and feeling embarrassed for him, realizing that I was not to blame for what he did or said. It was not my fault. He always made me feel guilty if things went wrong. He lost his wallet one night when he was out drinking and blamed me for it. I was tucked up in bed all alone, but felt guilty that I was not there to prevent him losing it.

These incidents happened all the time, and it was my choice to detach and let go of guilt and blame and start to live again. I can see now how crazy I had become in accepting these accusations and accepting this way of life as being 'normal'. When I was involved in the situation, I could not see the wood for the trees. I lived in a fog of fear, embarrassment, anger and resentment and could not see a way out.

When he insulted me, I now realize I had the choice to react and accept what he said as the truth or detach and see it was just his own insecurities. He could not press my buttons and make me feel guilty, insecure or inadequate any more. When I learnt to detach and balance myself, nothing could touch me. I was free of playing the victim. I did not have to nag, protect, feel hurt, abused, suffer and try to control or be controlled any more. I did not cause his drinking problem, I could not control him or it and I could not cure it. By freeing and letting go, I set myself free. I could stop rescuing and suffering his consequences and responsibilities. It was not my duty. I did not need his approval, only my own. It was time to take care of myself and live my own life.

As I grew up I saw my mother as a people-pleaser. She tried to make everyone else's life comfortable and okay except her own, never allowing herself to enjoy herself or spend money on herself as that was self-indulgent and bad, she thought. She feared my father and tried to please him constantly. Even if it were 110 degrees in the shade, she would cook a roast meal on Sundays because he wanted it. She tried to keep the house clean and perfect, fearing criticism from him. She did not have a happy life and I wanted to make sure I would not fall into that trap. I left home at the age of 15 and I tried to be different from her and put on a positive, smiling face but what I resisted, persisted. I found myself drawn into similar circumstances without realizing that my perception and conditioning, no matter how hard

I tried to be different, pulled me to hers and my reality of how life was. The same old pattern was established until I realized, accepted and then changed my patterns and beliefs.

Meditation helped tremendously, as the more I meditated, the more clearly I could see and recognize the old patterns I tended to fall into. By using visualization I saw the new me and developed a new belief about myself, realizing that I was worthwhile and I wanted and deserved a much better life for myself and my children than the one I had accepted. By changing my beliefs, I changed myself and then everything around me started to change.

The truth is that when I stopped trying to change and blame the people around me for my unhappiness, I found happiness, prosperity, love and peace of mind for and in myself. It did not appear on the outside before I had changed the inside.

In a few words ■ ■ ■ ■ ■ ■ ■ ■ ■ ■ ■ ■ ■

Being submissive, compliant and pleasing doesn't work to get the love and security you desire. It only draws to you a certain type of person you will never be able to please.

As long as you live to please, you will attract and be attracted to people who appear to be strong and seem to want to take care of you, but because they are also insecure and afraid of intimacy, they will control you. They won't appreciate you for trying to please them, because they don't want to give up their control, which is more important than loving you.

■ ■

Chapter 3

Disease – dis-ease with the body

The body is a wonderful machine that is wholly the product of the thought processes of the person who inhabits it. Every moment it paints the clearest, most intimate picture of all our feelings and attitudes. Every thought you have registers as an emotion within the body, an electrical spark that feeds each cell. Love, appreciation of unseen beauty, freedom of experience, patience, living in the now, allowing life to be; these are all attitudes that spark health within the cells of the body. Self-hate, self-denial, feelings of unworthiness, insecurity, jealousy, guilt, anger, failure, blame, resentment, sorrow; these attitudes degenerate the cells within the body to create illness and disease, for they are attitudes that alter life, that inhabit it. When your attitudes do not permit your life to be lived in freedom and in ease, the body will eventually mirror your attitudes and become diseased. The body will always reflect and represent a person's collective thinking.

When you do not cry enough to release your emotions you get a cold which helps you cry inside and release.

When you keep boredom inside, it turns into apathy.

When you keep grief inside, it turns into depression.

When you keep anger inside, it turns into hostility.

When you keep fear inside, it turns into worry and anxiety.

Sickness is not a punishment. It is the effect of a cause for which you were responsible. You can worry yourself into a state where you get an ulcer or any illness, because you allowed yourself to have tension instead of tranquillity, stress instead of serenity – you made yourself ill. If you look on disease as a punishment, it could only be you punishing you.

Anger, fear, guilt, boredom, grief and worry emotionally induce most illnesses; you get ill when the balance of your body is disturbed. You induce the imbalance. The body is a self-healing mechanism. Once the cause of the illness is removed, the body heals with enormous speed and restores the body to a balanced condition.

The body reacts to your attitude. There are attitudes that produce illness and there are attitudes that produce health; which ones you adopt are up to you. The body prefers to be healthy. To attain and maintain robust good health you must adopt a good attitude.

Repressed feelings and emotions affect your health. Playing the 'victim', smiling while you are stewing inside, not asking for what you want and feeling you don't deserve it, makes you ill. To be healthy and vital you must express your feelings, maintain positive emotions and believe you deserve to be healthy. If you have subconscious feelings of 'I'm not a good person', 'I deserve to be punished', 'I feel guilty', then the first step is illness to punish yourself, and then death as the permanent solution.

If you are doing work or leading a life you don't enjoy, your mind is constantly thinking, 'I wish I wasn't here,' and as your body does what the mind wants, it will try to get you out of being there through illness. Your mind makes your body and your body is a reflection of your thoughts. If fear, unexpressed emotion and anger consume you, your body will show it. The disease of the mind becomes the disease in your body.

Whenever you are quietly centred, at peace and thinking good thoughts about yourself and your environment, your metabolism changes. Your respiration, heart rate, blood pressure, blood sugar and glandular function changes. As your body relaxes, the mind relaxes; as the mind relaxes, your body relaxes more. In this state you can re-create your body. How materials of physical form respond to your thoughts and feelings, your weight, posture, the way you move, is determined by the quality of your thoughts. To change your physical form, change the quality of your thoughts.

> Let go of fears with love, laughter and tears and you will have health and vitality all your life

All illness is related to stress and distressed states of mind. Your state of mind affects your metabolism, your immune system, creativity, concentration and physical and emotional responsiveness. You can cure illness, fight addictions, control pain and realize all goals with the power of positive visualization.

Change your perception

Mind power based on excellence is an irresistible force. The only one thing on earth you can change is your mind and that is all you need to change. By changing your mind and attitude to self and others, you can change your life and transform your world. When you look at the world through a fog of fear, judgement and guilt, you see a world that is scary, shameful and lacking in worth. Any time you choose to change your perception, you can change that fog into a sparkling aurora and create a world of peace and beauty. At some level there is no 'out there', only an 'in here' and the world exists only to mirror you. Your subconscious mind takes on what you say and think about others and makes its personal truth from your perceptions. Everything you do, every thought you hold is ultimately about yourself. What you offer comes back to you. You reap what you sow and what you choose to see is what you get.

If you believe you have low energy, you will get colds and flu. Give yourself permission to have a healthy and energetic body and deal with damaging patterns of guilt, blame, resentment, criticism and anger at yourself. These are all thoughts that can be changed. You can choose to release the past and forgive everyone and yourself. When you approve and accept yourself completely as you are now, you will be free to live a healthy and happy life.

For any healing process to be successful, relaxation is essential. If you are tense, the healing energies have difficulty in flowing within you. Meditation, even for a few minutes a day, allows the body to let go and relax. It is not difficult or mysterious. Just sit quietly with closed eyes and take a few deep breaths. You do not have to force your body, it will automatically relax.

In a few words ■■■■■■■■■■■■■

Think happy thoughts and love and accept yourself as you are. You deserve to be healthy.

If things aren't going well and you feel unhappy, inadequate and angry, choose to learn from the situation but move on and choose to be happy and at ease with yourself.

You are responsible for every experience in your life, including illness. Every thought you have and what you speak is constantly creating your future.

■■■■■■■■■■■■■■■■■■■■■■■■■■

Chapter 4

Healing

Introducing universal energy or simply being a channel for love heals. God is love or universal energy. So when you channel love, you are acting as a channel for the Supreme Power. By this means, you can achieve many wonderful results, healing body, mind and spirit all at the same time.

When you are clear and have no resistance, you can allow this universal energy to come through you and create changes within. You will be strong and able to direct your own path. You will not be the victim of what other people want for you. You can own your own power and wisdom and be captain of your own ship. It is important that you do not allow the outside world to determine what is or is not possible for you and by staying in your own energy field you will be clear on what you want in your life.

When the energy centres in the body become clogged, it is because you have blocked certain things from your consciousness and pushed down your feelings. To keep these feelings down takes a great deal of energy. Sometimes you may say that you have a broken heart. Well it feels broken because you have closed off your feeling in the heart, communication gets stuck in the throat, and you can't say what you really want to for fear of hurting another person. Headaches often occur and you feel tired: sick and tired of being sick and tired. Your body slows down and energy leaves it. If your energy flow is slow and the lower body is cold or numb, you come to a sluggish halt. The body's response to stress and hypertension leads to depression. Your own life stress contributes to illness.

Love heals and dissolves fear, hurt and all negative emotions

When you take responsibility and take care of yourself you start to love yourself, and your body begins to regenerate and change. Meditation, breathing, allowing the universal energy to come in through your head and grounding are very effective in moving the energy flow and making you feel alive. You must be centred within to sustain a healthy and balanced energy field.

If the electrical currents are not able to flow freely through the body to sustain health within an uninjured cell or stimulate healing in a damaged cell, the body becomes old and decrepit or sick. If the energy centres are open and spinning freely, you will have a greater amount of energy being produced and moving through your body. If an energy centre is blocked, the energy flow is restricted. With more energy moving through the system you will look and feel younger and have more vital and radiant energy. When the frequency of the energy gets faster, your state of being becomes more refined and subtle, less dense. In the healing world you are operating in finer and higher frequencies or vibrations. When you run your energy through your body, you get a warm, tingly, spacey feeling.

Every person has within themselves their own uniqueness, and their own ideas of what they want to create for themselves in life. We are all free to experience this. The choice is yours, feeling alive or dull, living in fear and worry or living a life of love and freedom.

Getting in touch with your soul

If you are disconnected from your true potential for knowledge, love, understanding and wisdom, this is difficult. If you live a predictable life dominated by worry, stress and fear and believe that you are powerless to take charge of your own destiny, then you are not connected. If you open your heart and mind from its rigidity and lethargy in which many lie, you connect more and more to infinity and you understand that you are more than a physical body experiencing one meaningless lifetime. Air and light and food nourish the body and the soul is nourished and trained by your interior thought.

As your body is kept in a state of health and activity by exercise and worthwhile occupation, so every noble thought or wish expands the soul and gives it new vitality. Every mean desire, every ill wish for someone else, withers its delicate essence. You are a spirit with a body experiencing this world as part of your eternal journey of evolution through experience. To the happy person who is conscious of his daily expansion of the soul, there is nothing in this life that can grieve or distract him from happiness. Poverty, scarcity of money, friends, illness: all will be bearable. To whatever height of good fortune you may aspire, you shall never be spoilt by what is called success, as you know that in the evolution of the soul, this world's successes are mere splashes in the sea, not the sea itself.

There is a perpetual, passionate craving in the souls and lives of many for that internal peace and absolute content, which can only come when you are truly balanced with your energy running freely through you. Materialism does not, and can never still the hunger of the spirit in man for love and energy. Nothing temporal can soothe or console it, nothing can long delight it. In time, the best gifts the world can offer seem valueless, for when one spark of God's own essence of energy remains alight within it; it is impossible not to be vital and alive. You can feel the quick stirrings of a larger, grander life within you and with love and eagerness enjoy the wonders of the world. When you feel the first faint glimmer of the brightness that glitters when you allow yourself to open up to the universal energy flowing through you, your body will be healthy and free of any disease.

The knowledge of who we really are has been destroyed in most of the people on earth and we have become separate and disconnected from our source. But when you understand your true nature, power and worth, you will not give your power away to people with degrees who tell you to take this pill and that pill, this is what you must do to keep your life in order. Your body and mind will operate at their full potential, the human essence of absolute power, wisdom and purity.

With the ability to see beyond the things of this world, nothing temporal, however pleasant, brings any gratification or advantage to the soul. While stuffed into our small bodies without the healing influences of unselfish love and universal energy, the body starves and dwindles to a feeble flame. Operating from the lower astral frequency range you become disconnected from anything higher. Fear resonates at a low vibrational frequency, while love resonates at a high vibrational frequency. Feeling low-vibrational emotions as part of life's experience is okay but to be dominated by them and pulled down by them to depression is not. When these emotions control and become plugged into the lower dimension, you are open to being dominated by fear and can get stuck, sick and depressed. Our general state of health and being affects the rest of the world. When you change old rigid beliefs and attitudes, you change your body and state of being to a higher frequency and you can uplift yourself and other people.

Reconnecting with pure love

Consciousness is a series of interconnecting energy fields. There are emotions, intellect and spirit all resonating to different frequencies, and interpenetrating each other through a series of energy centres. It is through these energy centres that imbalances are passed to the mental and physical levels. Stress causes illness and you cannot think straight when you are emotionally upset. You become confused. From the heart you express love or hatred. When you are expressing love in its true and purest sense – unconditional, non-judgmental love – the heart opens. When you express hatred and close your heart, this causes a blockage and the energy cannot pass through your body.

We are all pure love and you cannot reconnect with your true self, pure love, while you are resonating with hatred or ill feelings. The only way to reconnect with pure love is to express and live pure love. To do this you must give up any desires you may have to control and dominate because this keeps you isolated from your source. When you live in fear you remain disconnected and limited from your own true self. Hatred, resentment, revenge, jealousy and judgement and fear have been stimulated in generous amounts in the way you have been brought up, programmed and moulded by your parents, teachers and religion. The fear of God is fear of self and fear of death and his judgement. Humanity is consumed and overwhelmed by fear. That is why you can be disconnected from who you are. You do not feel safe, loved and secure in a world of change and confusion. The truth is that God does not judge; there is no death as it is only your body that dies, your spirit lives on eternally.

When you live in fear you cut yourself off and find it hard to breathe. You feel separate, disconnected and suppressed from your source energy and intuition. Sexual energy, the creative force that is suppressed (if you believe that sex is bad), limits your human potential to manifest your desire and creativity. You become unplugged from the natural flow of the cosmic pulse. Low vibrational emotions cause imbalance and break the circuit, disconnecting you from the earth and universe. Most people have separated the head from the heart, the intellect from intuition and feeling, and the physical from the spiritual.

By allowing the universal energy to come through, you will find your own inner beauty suddenly transforms your outer appearance. Any emotional blockages or disease will dissolve to create a healthy and vital body. Your inner beauty starts permeating outwards to show the true being underneath. It was always there, only it was covered in so many layers of fear and disconnected from the universal source energy.

Feelings are your friends

To connect with your higher self, you may find that you have to have the courage to go through the wall of pain and allow your feelings to emerge. 'Don't open the can of worms,' I hear you cry. 'You never know what you will find.' But you clean your house, don't you? You delete old worn out programs on your computer, don't you? You replace them with newer updated versions? You clean out your old files, why not clean out your body. When you clean up your energy system, you move out energy and old pictures of emotional events that happened to you. It is only energy and energy can be moved. Left stuck in the body that toxic energy would slow you down and cause sickness.

Feelings are your friends and are there to help you. You know who you are already. I will just prod you to reawaken and let you remember who you truly are.

When energy enters your body from your feet, it moves upwards. If any energy centre is blocked, this energy will be blocked before traversing all the energy centres in the body. A healthy functioning energy centre will spin and a weak one will not seem to be spinning at all, which blocks energy flow. When all centres are aligned and functioning, a healthy process occurs and the energy can flow freely through your body.

A person suffering an emotional trauma or who was abused will have a large blockage in their body. A person who has not cried in ten years has usually gone through a severe depression or trauma and decided never to feel or trust again. They may even have forgotten why. They have just covered it up and got on with their lives. It is only later when they get ill and they have to slow down that they are ready to deal with the original pain or trauma. The body is such a wonderful machine that when you just have to keep going for survival, it continues to function for quite some time before it stops with disease.

My body did. My ex-husband tried to strangle me but I did not allow myself to feel the feelings, feel the shame and the humiliation that I truly felt inside. I could not allow myself the luxury as I had to work to support my two children. The cold money business had no room for such raw emotional outbursts. I shoved it all down and put on a brave front. I appeared as if nothing had happened, the pain was too viscous to deal with at the time. My body coped for some time; I put on weight to keep it all down, to protect myself from feeling the rage I felt. I became a robot, a good actress. It was only much later, five years later, that I allowed myself to feel, to let out the anger and hurt that I felt at that time. I took the emotional charge off the incident. I still have the memory, but the energy is no longer trapped in my body so I can tell the story as an observer and not feel the intense feelings that I had at the time. The emotional pain used to get stuck in my throat. That energy has moved out of my body. If it were still there, I would be really sick and perhaps have died by now. Let us take a look at why the dreaded feelings are good for us.

> Take your eyes off others and look at yourself instead

Feelings are good as they tell you how you feel, which helps to distinguish from what is appropriate for you to accept and what boundaries and limits you wish to set with people. If you did not have feelings, you could allow yourself to be abused on a regular basis and not be able to see it is not good for you and your body. Feel your feelings, integrate them and come into balance. The emotional blockages have to be discharged or dissolved for your energy to flow freely.

We see so many instances of people trying to be 'good', as in the case of a politician who has a clear life of distinction only to wreck it by one night out with a prostitute. A highly regarded psychologist ruined his whole career in a similar way. A big, buxom woman came to see him as a client. One day some force took over and in the middle of the session he sexually devoured her. He was struck off the register. Or there is the holy priest who molests little boys. What happened to these people? After so many years of 'containment', did their worst nightmare come out and wreck their perfect lives?

Don't suppress your emotions

I always had trouble dealing with hypocrisy as I saw it. People who pretended to be perfect and hid the truth of their dark side from everyone. Now I realize that when you suppress and do not deal with emotions, they can come up at the worst time. It is best to deal with them every day. If there is a backlog, deal with them when you are ready. It is wise to choose a workshop where it is safe to express your innermost feelings and let the raw emotions come out. Otherwise have some healings to deal with them. You will feel so alive and free and you will be able to express what you feel without any hesitation.

One lady I treated had throat cancer. She was adamant that she had a perfect childhood and upbringing and her mother was in the realms of being angelic. In the healing session we uncovered in her throat the old emotional wound of being sent to boarding school at the tender age of eight years old. She was put on a train and the sense of abandonment and fear were very real to her. She just could not understand why her mother did not love her any more and was sending her away. Once at school she had to shut off these feelings and be brave, to bite her bottom lip. Crying was unacceptable and she did not want to be called a cry-baby. Her body had closed off this traumatic memory for her and 45 years later she was left with cancer. By clearing out the electrical charge from this incident, the cancer disappeared. She was able to release her feelings and anger and resentment she felt towards her mother in a safe place and now has a much closer, loving relationship with her mother. Previously, she was quite distant and could not quite trust her mother entirely.

No one is bad! From the work that I have done giving healings and workshops, many people on the surface appeared perfect, but there was a mass of anger and resentment blocking them. The good news is that when all this comes out, like popping a pimple, they can love the person they are angry about because there is no emotional charge on the incident that caused the initial anger. The only reason people close off or cause family feuds is because they have got so out of touch with the true genuine feelings that they hate. Everyone who I have worked with ultimately loves their parents, friends and enemies and wants only the very best for them. When the emotional charge leaves, there is only pure love and the body can be light and free to express love. The only things in the way are fear and blocked emotions.

If you are cut off from your feelings, so it is all too easy to cut off from life and become just an empty shell. The energy system that should be feeding the internal organs may not be giving you the vital energy, the life force that you need to get through life. I noticed as a child that most people, because of the way we think, have their legs cut off from the rest of their body. We live in our heads most of the time and do not pay attention to the lower areas of the body. This energy and power, both physical and spiritual, that is located in the legs and thighs, is a very serious problem if you lose your connection to the earth and become ungrounded. You can always keep your connection to the earth by walking barefoot, otherwise you cut off the earth energy and become ungrounded.

When your body and spirit are connected as one, you have a real openness and simplicity that allows your energy to run freely. Using just the intellect, you may feel disconnected and invalidated and out of touch with your feelings. You are not up to speed and there is something wrong with you. It is a good idea to go barefoot whenever you can and let the earth energy run up your feet through your body.

One day I was scuba diving on Lizard Island on the Barrier Reef in Australia and it all became clear. I was playing with a giant cod and looking into his eyes of wonder. The dichotomy of connection and separation of people who lived on earth was evident.

In a few words ■ ■ ■ ■ ■ ■ ■ ■ ■ ■ ■ ■ ■ ■

Allowing the universal energy to flow through you is so important. If you don't run your energy, someone else will run it for you. In other words, if you do not take charge of your life someone will do it for you. Feel your feelings; they are your friends.

Imagine an earth energy that comes from the earth itself and enters your body through your feet. Bring the energy through your ankles, knees and into the core of your body.

See energy coming down from the source or the cosmos and feel it entering the top of your head and going down through your body.

■ ■

Chapter 5

Fitness and health

When you get other people's energy out of your space, you weigh less. You have to be senior in your space. You can pull it out by grounding. Everyone has to fend for him or herself and learn their appropriate lessons for themselves. Validate all your screw-ups. It is good to fail for that is how you learn. Your spirit had fun finding out what did not work for it. Beating yourself up is no good. You create and destroy so give all your cells permission to be in amusement for all your failures and see how the energy loosens up. The thick, serious energy gets broken up. Vibrate at fun and amusement and let it all go. Crying also lets out a lot of emotion and is good for the body.

I put on 50lbs of excess weight after my ex-husband tried to kill me. I had two children and had stopped exercising. My body was tormented, in shock and trauma that someone I had loved and trusted had tried to strangle me. I put on a brave face; I had to as I had children to take care of. My clients surely did not want to know. I was looking after them and their money. I took a back seat. My personal problems had no bearing on my professional position.

I had nightmares for two years after that. On the surface I carried on with gritted teeth. The weight kept the anger, resentment and toxic thoughts all covered up. Below the surface I was fuming with disbelief. How, why, did he do it? I knew he was an alcoholic but the assault on my body was immense. The pain I felt throbbed below the wads of extra padding, layers of fat I covered up with. It was not for five years that I seriously allowed myself to revisit the scene and look at it truthfully. I had such a charge on it, that when I did I felt the pain around my throat, which had cut off a lot of my creative energy in my arms and hands.

The grief that followed came out in sobs of fear and sadness. Instead of eating to cover up the pain, I allowed myself to sit and experience it. It was painful but it was, after all, only energy and energy can be moved. It released and suddenly the weight dropped off. It was like a ton was lifted from me and my body relaxed and let it all go. All the weight just dissolved when I knew I did not have to protect myself any more. I could take care of myself. My vitality bounded out again and I resumed who I was before the event.

Our bodies are amazing and I am still in awe of how they operate. Mine carried on, as this is what it needed to do for survival. When I was ready, I had made enough money and my children were okay, I could deal with the pain. Before that, I wasn't ready as I knew I had to carry on. I was afraid I would just fall to pieces and not be able to perform.

After I released the charge I had, I could talk about it and look at it from a detached point of view. My ex-husband was a tormented soul and I was in the way. That is all and I could now release all anger, resentment and a feeling that somehow I had deserved it.

Diet for life

Sick of dieting? How often have you gone on a diet, disciplined yourself and lost weight and then put it all back on again? Sounds familiar?

Do not drown your body in strong drink or burden it with too much food so you cannot hear the sounds of the spirit.

Do not overeat. Even the finest, most nutritious food available will spoil in your system if it is overeaten. Eat juicy, raw fruit and raw vegetables when the inclination to overeat surfaces. Raw vegetables will be particularly helpful. As you continue to eat these foods that are brimming with nutrients, the physiological basis for overeating will be removed. Eventually, you will be able to say, 'I used to overeat.'

Overeating is usually used to cover up negative thinking or something unpleasant. What happened to you as a child, when things went wrong and you were unhappy? Most likely, to comfort you your mother would say, 'Never mind, have a nice piece of cake,' or whatever was your favourite food. Do you overeat because of some fear, or because you want to prove some negative thought? The mind thinks and proves what it thinks, so whatever you think, your mind tries to prove it is right. So whatever you believe to be true is whatever you have created for yourself.

> Do not drown your body in strong drink or burden it with too much food so you cannot hear the sounds of the spirit

If you have the thought, 'I have been on so many diets, I have lost 10 pounds on this one, but it is too good to last, I am sure I will just put it on again,' to prove this thought, you will have to eat and put it all back on again. This will not change, until you change your negative thought into a positive one. If you have not dealt with past pain or trauma, your body will keep the protective fat until you release all the pain your body is carrying.

Next time you reach for the refrigerator door, stop yourself and allow yourself to feel your feelings. What are you thinking? Are you unhappy? What do you want to cover up? When I was pregnant, I had trouble sleeping I was so uncomfortable. I had heartburn and just could not get to sleep. I would roam around the house night after night and rob the children's sweets. Mars Bars were great. I felt better while I was eating them, but guilty later on. I felt miserable that I could not sleep, angry that everyone else in the house slept soundly and sorry for myself. To cover up, my pattern was to eat, and eat something sweet. I was a refrigerator-raider. To compensate for my body being so fat, I would eat to cover up my feelings and frustrations about my size. The more I ate, the worse I felt, and would eat yet more to cover up my unhappiness.

This escalates the problem, and until you get to the cause, and change your thoughts, nothing will work on a permanent basis. You create your own reality, and this includes the shape and size of your body. You must change your old patterns of thinking before you can create a new body. You cannot blame your parents, spouse or ancestors for your fat. Forgiveness and dropping your negative thoughts frees you from the past, frees you from your fears and frees you from your fat! If you believe you will never have a good body, you will not. The excess baggage you carry around in negative thoughts manifests itself in excess weight in your body. By changing your thinking and your attitudes, you can change your appearance and your weight. When you begin to love yourself, you can become the physically, beautifully slim self you want to be.

Ways to change your self-image

By using visualization with meditation, you can change your self-image to develop a positive concept of yourself and see yourself being a certain shape and size. You begin to love, not punish or go against yourself. The beliefs you have about yourself were passed down from your parents, who received disapproval when they were little. They failed to please their parents, who were controlling and demanding, and who withheld love and affection in order to control them. Your parents passed their beliefs down to you, and as a result you usually try to win their love and approval. When you fail to measure up to their 'expectations', bitterness and resentment towards them and people in authority is the result. Hostile and negative thought patterns are used to punish and beat us up regularly. 'Who would ever love such an ugly, fat person as me?' is a negative message and creates an ugly fat person. But you create your own reality, remember, and if you do not like your body the way it is now, you can re-create it. You must let go of the thoughts about yourself that made your body the way it is now.

It sounds easy, doesn't it? But remember how long you have been playing these old tapes – all your life – and it takes a little determination and time to build new messages. When you diet or fast out of sheer self-disgust or shame at the shape of your figure, you like yourself for a while, then the fat returns with the old patterns of thinking. If your fat is being used as protection or as a weapon against someone else, or to cover up some fears, it will return unless you get to the cause. When the cause has been dealt with, or acknowledged, the weight will drop off naturally, no matter what you eat. When you 'lighten up' your mind, you will 'lighten up' your body. It is as simple as that. No amount of dieting, fasting, depriving, jogging or exercise will do it permanently until you change your thoughts about yourself. You must eliminate negative and destructive thinking and instead give yourself a diet of forgiveness and love.

First you must be willing to be perfect and ready to stop punishing yourself and being angry with yourself. Are you ready to feel the fear that your fat is hiding, let go of your self-pity, and be free? If so, visualization in meditation will help you release the old thought patterns by visualizing yourself at your ideal weight, the shape you want your body to be. If you continue to do this twice a day, you will find your body changing. It is a good idea to put up a picture of you when you were slim, or if you never were, a picture of a figure you would like to have, and put your face on the top of it. Place it where you see it every day. Be kind to yourself. Give yourself a regular massage, it makes you feel prosperous. Treat yourself to a daily bubble bath. It feels luxurious.

Read the chapter on visualizations and affirmations to help you change your thoughts, which, in turn will change your body to the shape and size you want it to be. Being overweight is a reflection of your own self-hate. Try to feel what you hate yourself for. If you felt angry or ashamed at yourself, feel these feelings, then forgive yourself and love yourself. Love is light, moving and fluid. Hate is thick, dark and heavy. Excess weight is excess baggage, stuck energy, extra negativity and hate you are carrying around with you. You may be blaming or hating yourself, parents or spouse for being overweight. Let the feelings come to the surface and face them. When it has been a habit to blame for so long, it is hard to give up. Decide not to be a 'victim' any more. Forgive everything that anyone 'has done to you'. It doesn't matter any more.

> Let go, 'lighten up' your mind, and 'lighten up' your body with loads of love and laughter

Decide to be in charge and control your life and your own body to your own ideals, not your mother's or father's. You might fear happiness, and if you are using your fat for protection, it may scare you to feel too happy and too good about yourself. It will not feel safe for a while. You might feel more comfortable if you are miserable. Much safer. Realize that it is only safe because it feels familiar. 'Better the devil we know, than the one we don't.' This keeps people stuck in jobs, in marriages, and fat, until they can give up the old and move on to the new energy. Your negative thoughts are poison that you take every day. It is SAFE to give up hate, blame and to stop fearing your own good feelings. It is okay to be happy and to have pleasure. Give your body lots of sex and tender loving care. Keep yourself on a diet of love, and love and appreciate what you eat. What you love cannot hurt you. If you hate that piece of chocolate cake as you stuff it into your mouth, it will hurt you. It is not the cake; it is the feelings you have about the cake that will harm you.

The food you eat is part of your energy in motion, and if you force emotion to stagnate, your mind will stagnate together with lots of energy and enthusiasm. You become dull, tired and listless.

Be honest with yourself

We live in a society of control and phoniness. We may like to think we are sophisticated, but that, in fact, may sometimes mean phoniness. Every time you do something that you feel you do not want to do, but 'should' do, the mental and emotional processes of the mind are impaired because the mind could not let the body go. You are not using your body to its full potential.

How many times have you gone to a cocktail or dinner party with a bunch of stuffy, sophisticated people who ask you how you are, but are not really listening to your reply? They are looking over your shoulder to see whom they should talk to next. How often do you dress up for a ball or dinner party, sit there with a wise face, nod your head, but wonder what you are doing there talking about subjects you have absolutely no interest in? You sit there, stuffing yourself with food and drink because you do not want to stand out, do not want to offend, and tell yourself it is just for a couple of hours. It won't hurt.

It does hurt though. Acting sophisticated for that many hours a day, doing what you should be doing, rather than using your full potential to totally express yourself without concern for the result, dulls your energy. If you are totally expressing yourself and using your full potential, you will have no need to try and dominate anyone, suffer from illnesses, be angry and violent or use food, alcohol or drugs to escape from your sophistication.

The purpose of your life is not to modify your behaviour for the sake of society. You need to be your own authority, seek only your own approval and take responsibility for your own life. You need to be responsible, to be able to respond, which means not letting anyone tell you what the world is, what is right for you to do, or what is right for you to eat. That is your responsibility to yourself alone. Physically, nutritionally and mentally, you need to go beyond a belief system that is based on someone else's concept of expectations and 'That's the way it is'. For THEM maybe, but not necessarily for YOU. As long as you continue to buy into other people's belief systems, you lose your spontaneity, become dull and watch life rather than participate by risking to be alive.

If you feel you cannot behave the way you want to, you may modify yourself to fit in with society's expectations. You may be an enthusiastic person with an abundance of energy, a person who wants to live to your full potential, but everyone else is telling you to be quiet, it is not polite to laugh. Because they are putting their brakes on and are controlled, they try and control you into doing the same, to conform. Pretty soon, if you slow down and conform to meet other people's expectations, you do not risk expression, and soon you run down and lose your ability to perform at your peak level. Your body cannot express the mind, because the mind cannot direct the body.

Maintaining your health

As long as you question, compare and hold on to thoughts without acting upon them, your health, radiance and vitality sag. When you hold on to a thought, it becomes like a caged animal. The thought has vitality, but you are not allowing it to use that vitality. You have taken away its freedom of expression. When you hold on to resentments and judgements and are self-righteous, you hold on to your opinions and in turn your judgement blocks your spontaneity and impairs your metabolism. You become malnourished.

Spontaneous activity, without question and without concern for the result, will give you joy and enable you to give joy. Nothing can stagnate and that energy has a flow directed outwards from the body and you radiate energy. Expression and radiance are enhanced by the full involvement of body, mind, heart, and spirit, and that will keep you healthy.

As you continue to transform yourself and move to higher and higher energy levels, you evolve through your involvement. When you are fully involved, you are not at work, you are expressing.

In a few words ■■■■■■■■■■■■■■

The more potential you express, the less stagnation you will endure. Learn to be a warrior instead of a worrier. The more your energy is moving, the more power it has, and the greater your vitality.

When you accept responsibility for yourself and do what your higher self tells you what you can do, and you do not listen to outside authorities telling you what you should do, you develop your full potential and your energy increases. You can express yourself at any time.

If you stay stuck in what you think you should be doing through guilt, fear, and inadequacy, then moving on to the unknown will scare you, but if you stay, you will lose your zest for life, become dull and your health will suffer.

■■■■■■■■■■■■■■■■■■■■■■■■■

Chapter 6

Lighten up
with laughter

Through all the difficult times in my life my good sense of humour and ability to laugh at myself have got me through. Laugh and the world laughs with you. Cry and you cry alone. Misery loves company but nine times out of ten you will find no one to share it with.

By knowing how to laugh at myself, I know I will never cease to be amused. One of the best things about laughter is that it breaks through the tendency each of us has to take our values and ourselves too seriously. It breaks down the roles we play and liberates the self that is locked within. It is our tendency to identify with our own self-created image, fears, beliefs and assumptions that takes us away from the joy that we believe is normal for each of us to feel.

The scientific press now confirms what was expressed in Chapter Two, that repressing feelings and negative emotions, such as anger, resentment, fear and despair, are major factors in the development of serious illness, from cancer to coronary heart disease. Scientists have charted direct pathways between mind and immunity via anatomical connections that link the brain directly to organs such as the spleen and the thymus gland. They have shown that hormonal secretions induced by emotions and thought patterns create a second pathway between mind and body which is carried in the blood, and there is strong evidence that excess adrenaline from high levels of stress can significantly depress the body's immune system. Many scientists are investigating the bio-chemical changes brought about by positive emotions and are encouraging their use as tools for health and healing. Researchers now find that laughter, relaxation, meditation and hope not only produce beneficial changes, such as lowered heart rate and breathing, they can even improve the way the body responds to stress hormones and bring about a shift in your perception of potentially stressful situations. You can look on them as challenges rather than as problems you cannot deal with or solve. This is a vital attitude in preserving and enhancing the health of the mind and body.

The benefits of laughter to your feelings are both psychological and physiological and have been documented. The act of laughing releases beta-endorphins, chemicals in the brain that act as the body's own painkillers. It was William James, a nineteenth-century philosopher, who said, 'We don't laugh because we are happy, we are happy because we laugh.' The reason laughter produces happiness is physiological. Laughter causes the facial muscles to move up and down, which stimulates the thymus gland, the master control for our immune system. When that gland is activated, it functions better and sends out waves of 'killer T-cells' that quite literally destroy anything negative in their path. Laughter loosens us up, massages our internal organs and causes loss of control, which is why so many people are afraid of it.

In 1964 Norman Cousins was one of the first to use laughter

to heal himself of ankylosing spondylitis, a degenerative and presumably fatal disease of the spinal connective tissues. He used lots of vitamin C and Marx Brother's movies. He cured himself.

The health benefits of laughing begin with the dilation of the cardiovascular system, which enables you to keep your flexibility. Initially, when you laugh, your heart rate and blood pressure go way up, then drop down below the norm. That is wonderful for those constricted blood vessels that cause high blood pressure. If you laughed as much as children, you could have the same heart rate and blood pressure as them.

Accept your life and be happy. You can't get out of life alive!

Next, as the diaphragm convulses in laughter, the internal organs get massaged, which is what keeps them functioning. It is also why sometimes your sides may hurt when you have just gone through a bout of unaccustomed laughing. As massive amounts of air are gulped in, your blood is highly oxygenated. The air that is expelled during laughter has been clocked at seventy miles per hour, so we know our respiratory system is getting a tremendous workout. We also lose muscle control, which relaxes the musculoskeletal system. The brain produces hormones called beta-endorphins, which reduce pain, and our adrenal glands manufacture cortisol, which is a natural anti-inflammatory that is wonderful for arthritis.

Laughter and a good sense of humour cure, in a world that tends to measure health not as joyous energy and creativity, but in terms of cholesterol levels and blood pressure. A life that sparkles with laughter is not only good for you because it feels good, it can also help you look after the state of your blood pressure, cholesterol levels and immune system far better than medical care drugs, which can have deeply worrying side effects. The worst of laughter's side effects is happiness and joy. When you laugh, you shed feelings of judgement, self-pity and blame.

Your perception shifts and you come to know another level of consciousness. Laughter deepens breathing, expands blood vessels, increases circulation by bringing more oxygen to your cells, speeds tissue healing and helps stabilize bodily functions.

I spend a great deal of my time laughing. It is a free expression of human vitality and creativity. If you do not know how to laugh, try to rediscover the art of being silly like a child. Watch how children laugh and play and have fun. Try and spend time with people who make you laugh and look for books and see films that make you laugh.

Never be afraid to laugh

A conspiracy of sorts exists against laughter. If you are laughing, it is hard to control people. The first thing a dictator does is get rid of the comedians. You do not have to tell jokes or use other devices to prompt responses. You do not have to make people laugh, just create places where people can laugh and feel safe. It helps people not to take anything seriously. People who are ill or recovering from surgery can use laughter to step back from the situation, get the big picture and 'play with their pain'. The technique works with mental 'pain' too, and depression.

Many people do not know how to laugh and it annoys them to see other people being joyful and happy. Don't take any notice of them. It is their problem not yours. Laughter is a release and besides having fun, a way to remain healthy. Most of us have been taught as children that when we laugh too much we have lost control. We are told, 'Control yourself, it is unladylike to laugh out loud.' It comes from fear, fear of being out of control, and when most people hear someone else laughing loudly, they feel nervous and uncomfortable.

Most people are afraid of being ridiculed for laughing, being called silly and not looked at as responsible adults. Our laughter may be judged; some people snort, whoop with laughter or guffaw, wet their pants or start to cry. This isn't exactly decorous social behaviour. Usually, women laugh more than men do, because they are not as afraid of losing control and looking silly.

Laughter has taken its knocks over the years, though. Plato maintained that laughter was improper for dignified men. Lord Chesterfield, the eighteenth-century English statesman, described it as the 'Mirth of the mob, who are only pleased with silly things.' Shelley concluded, 'There can be no entire regeneration of mankind until laughter is put down.' The attitudes of these antagonists of laughter still prevail, and as a result society suffers. But laughter, and other emotions like grief and rage, are cathartic, and repressing them causes untold damage.

The solution? Learn to laugh, cry and grieve. Most of us have not been allowed to express these emotions. For many years, I have encouraged people to laugh, cry and undergo other so-called cathartic processes to discover and release pent-up emotions, like depression, guilt and hostility. Expressing emotions to heal yourself is very valuable, as you don't hold on to sad toxic feelings in your body and repress them. By expressing, you deal with events because you don't hold on and keep them inside you. It is what every infant knows innately.

The best way to find amusement is to ground. Close your eyes and create a grounding connection from the base of your spine to the centre of the earth. Say hello to yourself inside your head. Funny things help us find amusement, but it is actually a vibration of energy, not a joke or something funny. Visualize a ball of energy that represents amusement and see if there are any colours or symbols. Bring the ball down into the top of your head. Let the colour of that energy float through your body.

In a few words ■ ■ ■ ■ ■ ■ ■ ■ ■ ■ ■ ■ ■

In dealing with sick people, some of them dying, it helps them to be able to laugh about their pain.

■ ■

Taking your power and affinity

Your body takes certain energies and issues very seriously. Traumas from past lives may remind it of its mortality. The spirit that is running your body is in amusement and having fun, it is just your body that is in pain. To be able to laugh a full-bodied, throat-to-belly, four-octave series of guffaws, hearty and warm and *lilting* and unavoidably, irresistibly infectious is healing.

That is the way all laughter starts, by playing with pain. Laughter is not attached to happiness. In order to trigger laughter you have to trigger your pain. We laugh loudest when we correctly pinpoint the source of our pain. Don't wait to be happy to laugh; laughter makes us happy. We should all get a daily dose of laughter. You can say, 'Ha, ha, ha, hee, hee, hee,' out loud to get started.

When I was going through my divorce, I used to meet my girlfriends for a drink and a laugh. It felt so good to laugh at the dreadful situation I had found myself in, which certainly was not without its ups and downs. My friends asked me how I could possibly laugh at the situation. My reply was, 'If I didn't laugh at it, I would cry; besides, it felt good to laugh at the pain.' Laughing and crying are both healing. When you laugh or cry, your life lightens tremendously. You have an emotional shift, and the problems you have do not seem quite so bad. It helps to relieve the tension. All laughter comes out of stress, tension and pain and since 95 percent of pain is psychogenic (originates in the mind), laughing can relieve physical and emotional hurts.

Let go, let be. Lighten up with laughter

Comedians mostly learn the value of laughing growing up in a rough neighbourhood. In order to survive, 'If you kept the bully laughing, there was no way he could beat up on you!' Most comedians realize this and use the connection between laughter and pain. When people laugh, they are playing with their pain. Laughter does not take work, at least not head work. Laughing is not the same as showing a sense of humour. A sense of humour is highly individual, unique to each person, but laughter is universal, and it is one of the most basic and safest human responses.

If you want to be a thinking, caring and communicative person, you have to take the risk and laugh. Once you laugh, you begin to cry and rage and storm as you once did when you were a child. Children heal so much faster than adults because of this. A study shows children laugh once every four minutes. Girls love to giggle with their girlfriends. They all get together and love it, and giggle and giggle, releasing all fear and tension. It is so sad that because of conditioning we still maintain stiff, formal facades to keep the tension and fear locked up inside of us. This is only because we were taught by adults and teachers to keep control.

I recommend a weekly get together for a 'laugh meditation'. You do not say anything at all. You arrive and just laugh for 45 minutes and then leave. It releases a backlog of tension and fear and you are in a safe place to do it. Laughter is very contagious and even if you have trouble laughing, you will soon be splitting your sides with glee.

Let loose, liven up

Laughter does not come from happiness, it comes from tension, stress and pain. Certain laughter balances the body chemicals produced by fear. A different kind of laugh will balance the internal chemistry of anger. These painful emotions produce stress chemicals in our bodies, but nature has given us natural cathartic processes to rebalance those chemicals. They are processes like laughing, crying, sweating, yawning, trembling and raging. Not just laughing, but all forms of catharsis are 'good for the health'.

Letting go and getting in touch with feelings about something specific is the beginning of the road to catharsis. Painting is a process of confronting yourself, as is writing or any other creative effort. You must face yourself over and over again as you confront an empty canvas or a blank page.

Cathartic therapy involves four basic steps. first, you get in touch with your feelings. Second, you release them through catharsis, processes such as laughing, crying or allowing yourself to get into a rage. Third, you rethink the situation or the experience associated with the feelings, which now has become possible because the chemical balance in your body allows you to think more clearly. Then, finally, you take whatever sensible action is appropriate, re-framing the content to see it from a new or different perspective.

In a few words ■ ■ ■ ■ ■ ■ ■ ■ ■ ■ ■ ■ ■ ■

Laughter without ridicule is a cosmic juice; connecting and bonding. Though not accepted in the West, in the East we have a Laughing Buddha.

It is said that 15 minutes of laughter is equal to 8 hours of meditation. Why not try it. Nature gave us a natural way to release tension, stress and pain. I would rather take the natural, happy way. It costs less and is much more fun!

We all have a tendency to take life so seriously. We think we must make great effort and exert ourselves in one way or the other in our search for spiritual fulfilment, making it complicated and hard, when the truth is really so simple. You are the answer; you are love, the purpose and the truth.

■ ■

Chapter 7

Meditation for
health

More and more business executives and people under stress are finding an increasing inability to wind down and relax. Their ratios of work and rest become top-heavy and play becomes the expendable part of the equation. Long periods of stress exhaust the brain, our ability to concentrate fails and restful sleep begins to misfire. Emotions are unbalanced, leading to depression, irritability, irrationality, lethargy or hyper-activity, and when the brain malfunctions, the body behaves abnormally too.

One way to cope with the pressures of life is meditation or going within. The degree of relaxation experienced during meditation is deeper and more beneficial than that achieved during sleep. It has been scientifically proven that during periods of total relaxation, alpha waves are emitted by the brain. This induces an 'alpha state' whereby the brain is alert to surroundings and, at the same time, is completely relaxed in a state of 'heightened awareness'. Sporadically, even more complex waves

– theta – are emitted. These are responsible for the highly creative and imaginative period experienced prior to sleep. Achieving alpha or theta states is not easy; they do not automatically come with sleep. (This is why severe stress sufferers often wake after eight hours and yet still feel tired.) Alpha and theta waves can, however, be induced regularly through meditation and at will by the practised meditator. Once mastered, these states have the power to calm the mind and relax the body, and relieve the symptoms of stress. As well as a reduction in stress-levels, other benefits include increased perceptiveness, heightened creativity and a greater sense of well being and an ability to enjoy life outside work more fully.

You can do meditation privately or in groups. It balances your being and you are getting in touch with who you are and what you think. In addition, creative visualization or imagery can be used to visualize yourself the way you want to be or in situations you wish to be in, creating your own reality. Your subconscious is able to dictate your performance in life, and through positive or negative thinking you can program yourself for success or failure.

In practical terms, meditation allows the normally dominant part of the brain – the left, or rational side – to switch off. Once this has happened, the brain unscrambles, relaxes and the more intuitive, creative right side of the brain engages. Learning to do this takes a little time as instinct tells the right brain to remain constantly alert. Practitioners use various techniques to prepare the brain to disengage; they go through a series of set rituals such as lighting candles, to set the scene, or playing specific pieces of music. After one or two weeks of practice, the process becomes automatic, and the time needed to achieve relaxation becomes shorter. It is possible to meditate successfully for just one minute, which emphasizes quality rather than quantity. Westerners often find disengagement of the brain to be difficult. We tend to think that if our brain is not fully active, then we should be dead.

Beginners are taken on a form of imaginary mystery tour, along a beach, through a forest or to some form of tranquil scene, which is a beautiful place in nature. The establishment of the tranquil scene provides you with an environment of reinforcement of your natural state of peace. It is used to balance your energies when you are under stress, or to provide new energy to sustain you between long hours without sleep. It also happens to be the most delightful place you have ever been.

Meditate to allow the jewel in you to shine through

I have used Alpha Meditation for over 20 years now and find it very effective. Originally, I did it to relieve stress, and then to get answers to problems; I had specific goals and I visualized them being successful. I now come from a more centred place inside that makes me feel calm, safe and secure, knowing that whatever happens is okay, because I am okay, and I have the choice of reacting in whatever way I choose. Whatever anyone does to me, or whatever happens to me is okay, because the only thing that matters is how I deal with it, and by taking responsibility for it and choosing to react in a positive way, it is ultimately my choice to be happy or unhappy.

The effects of meditation

With so much stress and negativity around, meditation has become an important tool for people from all walks of life. Anyone who lives or works in a hectic urban environment knows how essential it is to get away from it all occasionally.

You can go anywhere you like with meditation, it does not matter where you are. You do not have to drop everything and go on holiday (although that can be important too sometimes). You can find the peace and regeneration you need within yourself by practising meditation. It teaches concentration, focus and involvement and gives you extra energy. Lack of energy and vitality are the most common complaints of otherwise healthy people. We all have a great deal more potential energy than we ever use.

Meditation enables you to tap into this universal energy and it permits access to more of your human potential. In this way it enables you to experience oneness with life and you feel the security and peace of 'coming home'. It is simply a time for you to be quiet with yourself. A going within to find, to recover, to come back to something of yourself you once dimly and unknowingly had and have lost without knowing what it was or where or when you lost it. You were born with it but somehow along the way you felt separated from it. You may call it access to more of your human potential or being closer to yourself and to reality, or moving nearer to your capacity for love and zest and enthusiasm or your knowledge that you are a part of the universe and can never be separated from it, or your ability to see and function in reality more effectively.

To effect clear awareness, you must be conscious and clear with yourself. You are creating your reality with every thought that you think. Are you constantly aware of what you are thinking? Few people are! There are only three kinds of thought: past, present and future. The more effort you spend on keeping your conscious thought in the 'present' or 'now', the more brilliantly clear your spiritual and psychic awareness will be.

How to meditate

How you meditate depends on you. It is beneficial to sit cross-legged or in a lotus position to have the energy move around the body, but this is by no means essential. Most find it best to meditate in a sitting position so as to remain alert; lean against a wall if you like, or sit on a cushion so that your pelvis is tilted slightly forwards. You can also lie down, but as this is associated with sleeping, it is not ideal. Try always to meditate in the same room as this gathers the energy and becomes a special place.

Meditation takes you to a deep state of relaxation coupled with a wakeful and highly alert mental state. Make sure that you are safe from disturbance. Take the phone off the hook and lock the door. You will be aware of everything around you and can react in an emergency, but ideally you want peace and quiet as any sound will disturb you and make you jump.

- Become aware of the way you breathe as conscious breathing helps you connect with your physical sensations and to amplify them. As you become more sensitive to the flow of your breath, you'll be able to direct and breathe into that part and create tingling sensations of warmth and being alive.

- Close your eyes and relax. Breathe in a slow and conscious way, with full attention focused on the inflow and outflow of breath. When you concentrate on your breath, your attention is taken away from your thought processes, which quietens the mind. This creates an inner silence and you go on an inner journey using your breath as a vehicle. You will have much more clarity and sharper sensory perceptions if you practise this regularly. When you inhale air or prana, you inhale the universal life force, and the deeper you inhale the more you absorb and the more vitality and energy you will have.

- Thoughts usually preoccupy us so much that breathing remains shallow, which blocks the awareness of other things that are happening. We live in our minds, sustain ourselves on a minimal flow of air and as a result operate a low level of awareness and energy.

- When you close your eyes, focus on your breathing rather than your thoughts. As you inhale, feel the air coming into your nose to your chest and stomach. Be aware of the gentle rise and fall of your stomach as you inhale and exhale.

- Do not concentrate and try too hard to stop thinking. Thinking does not go away easily. Let your mind think if it leads you to thoughts, but just notice them and go back to your breathing.

In a few words   ■ ■ ■ ■ ■ ■ ■ ■ ■ ■ ■ ■ ■

*It is a good idea to meditate twice a day, say at 8am
(which will give you a clear and focused mind for the
office or daytime activities), and 6pm (to vitalize and
give you energy for the evening).*

*Having children to organize and a business to run I
used to fall asleep at dinner parties after a hard day's
work, but now have much more vitality and find I need
much less sleep than before. Half an hour's meditation is
equal to two hours sleep, so do not make the excuse that
you do not have enough time.*

*By meditating you will find you are more efficient at
work, you are more patient and loving with the family,
and friends will wonder what have you been doing to
yourself.*

*You will be more relaxed and content within yourself
and find you can remain more balanced and centred in
disturbing situations. Situations or people can do
anything to you, but as long as you do not react, you
remain centred and in control. If you react with anger,
abuse or allow yourself to get upset, you have lost your
focus and balance.*

*As you discipline yourself to meditate, you find yourself
more at home in the universe, more at ease with your
fellow man and yourself and feel less anxious and
hostile.*

*You are more able to work towards your goals and life's
work, which is something we all love to do, and are not
just earning money to survive. This is very stressful.
When you are doing something you love to do, the
money will come.*

■ ■

Creative
visualization

Creative visualization or imagery is working with the mental energy field to create your world by the direction of your energy. You and you alone create your own reality, so instead of letting things happen to you, why not direct and create what you want to happen to you? There are no limitations – whatever you desire, you can have; whatever you want to do, you can do. You are what you think you are, so if you are constantly putting yourself down and telling yourself you cannot do things or you do not deserve, then you will block off the energy to prove yourself right and will not achieve your goals. We are all capable of achieving anything we wish. But the reason most of us do not is that we let the negative thoughts and energies prevent us from it.

If you believe something is possible, it is. first of all you must define your goals. Write out in detail what you want and in your meditation see it happening. Do not worry about how you will get there, it is only your negative conditioning that stops you.

The world as you see it is a reflection of what you are. You are a living picture of yourself, your feelings and your conscious thoughts. Attitudes and beliefs construct your world. If you believe your life is enjoyable, it will be. Turn the negative into a positive.

It all has to do with the way you perceive situations. We all see it differently. For example, if you got sacked from your job, you may have thought the world would end, you are not good enough, you are a failure, etc. etc. But on the larger scale of things, if you look back, you might see that it opened other opportunities that would not have been there if you had not been free. Everything that happens is for a purpose. You have to grow and by hanging on to the old, where it is comfortable and safe, you will not grow. By risking moving out of your safe comfort zone to new horizons, you expand and achieve.

Some of the limiting beliefs you may have about yourself are:

1. Life is a struggle.
2. My body is fat and inferior.
3. I am a victim of circumstances.
4. I am not in control of my life.
5. I am at the mercy of my father/mother, husband/wife or boss.
6. I am at the mercy of my past.
7. I am helpless because of my karma.
8. People are basically bad and out to get me.
9. I have the truth and no one else has.
10. I will get sick and frail as I grow old.
11. Money is evil.
12. I am not good enough.
13. I do not measure up.

14. I am a bad father/mother.
15. No one loves me.
16. I do not deserve love.

There are so many limiting beliefs and things and they all serve to block energy and prevent you from achieving what you want to achieve. It is hard to change your beliefs; the negative beliefs are so strong and hard to remove. But one way I found successful is by using creative visualization in alpha meditation.

Alpha meditation is a relaxation process wherein the brain activities are slowed in order to rest the body and recharge its energies. During this process the mind is turned inwards and external stimulation reduced to a minimum. Alpha refers to a rate of brain activity. As the brain is an electrical instrument, its energy cycles at various rates. During normal day-to-day situations while awake the brain cycles at rates above 14 cycles per second (cps). This is referred to as beta brain waves. During sleep, the brain slows and varies the cycles at different times during the sleep period. These variations are alpha (7-14 cps), theta (3.5-7 cps) and delta (below 3.5 cps). During alpha cycle rates, dreaming is also experienced. Alpha meditation is aimed at reducing the brain waves to the alpha level, yet the individual remains fully conscious. In this state you are able to create and explore dreams and discover the causes of many of the problems and situations that occur during normal waking hours. This state of alpha also provides the ability to control stress, enhance memory, improve health and re-energize the entire body and mind.

Use alpha meditation to control stress and enhance memory

Meditation for creative visualization

An effective way to meditate is to visualize and create a workshop in your mind in which you can see yourself as you want to be, see yourself achieving and having the things you want or see a relationship being worked out. Include in the workshop a stage, lift, a desk with two chairs, a screen and a full-length mirror. When you meditate, see yourself in a tranquil scene to relax you. This provides you with an environment of reinforcement of your natural state of peace. It is used to balance your energies when you are under stress, or to provide new energy to sustain you between long hours without sleep. It also happens to be the most delightful place you have ever been. During the years, this tranquil scene may change in line with your own development by itself, so do not force it. It may be a mountain scene or a beach, a babbling brook or a city street. Whatever it is, just go with it and feel yourself being there.

The workshop is a place in the mind that is built by your imagination, visualization and emotions. The shape and style of your workshop can be anything you desire that gives you a feeling of freedom, joy and security; it may be a bubble, a pyramid, a crystal cave, a log cabin, a thatched hut on a beach, a castle or anything you like. The possibilities are endless.

- To start, begin with deep, relaxed breathing, letting the breath flow deep into your chest and stomach and then slowly out. Let it go deep inside and enjoy the cleansing power of the breath without having to make an effort.

- Imagine yourself moving through a light chamber on an escalator of red, the colour of rubies, orange, yellow, emerald green, sapphire blue, amethyst purple, indigo, and then surrounded by gold light. Feel yourself becoming a totally balanced person, emotionally, spiritually, in perfect health, loving and financially abundant.

- After you have relaxed in the tranquil scene, see yourself going down five steps. You will feel yourself going down. There you will see a waterfall to cleanse your entire negative thoughts and energies. Then you can enter your workshop and imagine yourself on the screen.

○ As you look at yourself, see and feel yourself becoming the person you would like to be and realize you are now that person. Know that you will be successful at anything you want to do.

○ Then let a memory or feeling arise behind your closed eyes – a visualization from the past or something you may wish for in the future.

○ Remain as a passive spectator, relaxed and receptive, seeing as many details as possible. Imagine the colours, smells, sounds and taste.

○ Step into the picture and become the actor in the scene rather than a spectator. Continue your deep breathing and feel your emotions of that time in your heart. Feel them intensely and as directly as you can. Let all the emotions connected to the experience resonate within you. You may feel joy, happiness, excitement or whatever sensation you have – just go with it.

○ Let your imagination go and if you experience something unpleasant, recreate the scene into something pleasant. See yourself letting go, childlike and playful.

○ If you want to adjust your weight, see yourself at your ideal weight. If you want to stop smoking, see yourself without a cigarette. See yourself enjoying abundance and security. If you lack confidence or feel powerless, claim your own power and see yourself confident and assertive. Feel yourself becoming a totally balanced person, emotionally, spiritually and in perfect health. See yourself being joyful and happy surrounded by your friends and loved ones. See what you want, what you want to have and what you want to achieve.

○ Gradually return to the present, letting your breathing slow down. Release the memories, images and feelings as you exhale. When you return to your normal waking state, review your meditation.

Repeat this every morning for 5-15 minutes and then let it go for the rest of the day. The secret of manifestation is being willing to let go and not have it. It is the ability to clear your mind and reprogram your consciousness.

In a few words   ■ ■ ■ ■ ■ ■ ■ ■ ■ ■ ■ ■ ■

You can create whatever you want. There are no limitations, only the ones you place on yourself. Be careful what you visualize — you will create it for yourself. You are the writer, producer, director and star of your reality. Make sure it is one of glee!

■ ■

Chapter 9

Manifestation

Most of us do not even know what we want or what we want to achieve, where we want to go and what we want to do. If we do not think we deserve, then we will not achieve. Goals give a direction and purpose. They give interest, enthusiasm, and more energy to make life exciting and sometimes even magic. By setting and writing down goals you create a powerful, psychological, spiritual, emotional and magic force. You become aware of and do the things you need to do to achieve, and then your goals come to you. Be careful what you ask for though, because you will get it!

When you leave your heart open, know and surrender to your goals, they work on the subconscious mind, which is in balance. The conscious mind is usually full of all the negative reasons why you cannot achieve and do not deserve to have what you desire. When your goal is absorbed into your subconscious mind you act the right way automatically without blocks, and go straight to the goal. You can turn everything into a goal, including how to solve a problem or a relationship worked out with friends, children and spouse. Your goal may be to have fun and be happy; to lose or gain weight; to stop worrying; to detach from family situations; to attract a new man into your life; to experience unconditional love; to enjoy sex or to forgive or be forgiven.

There are no limits on what you can ask for but do add 'for the highest good of all concerned', and then if it is not meant for you, you will not get it.

You can make owning a new car, house or jewellery a goal, or making vast quantities of money a year, or a certain amount of money in your bank account to give you the financial security you need to do other things. But do not just put down that you want more money; state how much, be precise!

Surrender to your desires and write on a piece of paper:

What you want to be.

What you want to do.

What you want to have.

Then ask yourself:

Why can't I have this item?

What is my attitude on this item?

What am I afraid will happen if I do not have this item?

What have I read or heard about this item?

What do others say about this item?

What emotions do I connect with this item and who has this item?

••

This gives you focus and directs your energy. Until I learnt about manifestation I did not have any goals. I thought life just happened. I have used this method for the last 20 years and it works. I now realize that when you know your goals, you can direct your energy into achieving them. I make a list and every six months cross off what I have achieved and then make a new one.

> To manifest your goals, you must first know what they are and then set them

When you visualize what you want for 5-15 minutes per day in meditation and then let it go, your subconscious mind will work towards getting what you want. You have put out what you want and your mental energy will work towards getting it for you.

You can use your mental visionary power to transform the energy around you from negative to positive energy and you can create whatever you wish.

By practising this you are experiencing the rapid co-creation and manifestation of wishes and desires. You are now taking the responsibility for yourself on a much more spiritual level. You are realizing that you have complete dominion and power over aspects of your world. Your smallest wish is the command to your higher self for manifestation.

In a few words ■ ■ ■ ■ ■ ■ ■ ■ ■ ■ ■ ■ ■ ■ ■

Creativity is a process of manifesting in a tangible form, the formless energy of the universe. Every individual is a channel for this energy.

The history of humanity is a record of expression. Mankind has been creating himself and his environment. An open heart is essential in any creative process.

■ ■

Steps for manifestation

1. Achieve a daily state of conscious mental silence.

2. Set your goal.

3. Create an affirmation and repeat it twice a day.

4. During meditation, visualize your goal and see yourself doing it or having it.

The necessary elements for complete manifestation are as follows:

1. Desire: is your heart aligned with your desire?

2. Belief: do you truly believe this goal is reachable?

3. Acceptance: are you truly willing to receive the abundance, peace and prosperity this dream will bring to you?

4. Is it for the highest good of all concerned? If it is not, is it better you do not have it?

If you are getting any resistance from yourself in honestly answering any of these questions, then you are not yet in tune with your higher self. Continue to practise a state of conscious mental silence (moment of the NOW, or meditation) in the areas you are experiencing resistance.

Worksheet for discovering your goals

Complete this worksheet as honestly and in depth as possible. Then write your 'dream' story in the first person, present tense. This story and assignment is to be for you and your energy only. Do not share it.

Fantasies and creative ideas

List any ideas, plans or dreams for the future, or any creative ideas that come to you, no matter how 'crazy' they may sound.

Success list

List everything you are now, or have ever been successful at or have done successfully in your life. Include everything, not just work. List everything that has real meaning to you.

Self-appreciation list

List all the ways you can think of to be good to yourself; things that are for your own satisfaction, large or small.

Dream Story

Create a story describing how you see your life being one year from now. Include your income, place of residence, type of work and relationships.

Chapter 10

Affirmations and empowerment

To overcome negativity and to come to a life full of power, you must gradually displace negative programming and inner weaknesses by concentrating on your positive strengths. Affirmations are a way to help you change and reprogramme. To affirm means to say things positively and declare them firmly to be true; this is empowerment, to give the ability to permit.

An affirmation is almost like a mantra. It does not matter if what you are affirming is not true yet, because by repeating an affirmation over and over again, it becomes embedded in your subconscious mind, and eventually becomes your reality. You can repeat affirmations or write them over and over again. Eventually, your subconscious will accept your affirmation as reality, your self-image will improve and whatever you affirm will be true. You make it true by creating your own new reality. Affirmations help you to change the rules, change your old messages and insert new beliefs to give yourself new abilities.

But if you ask for success and then prepare for failure, you will receive the situation you are preparing for.

If you express an affirmation of that which you wish to achieve or have happen but do not really believe it, then during your free hours you will work out plans on what you will do when you fail, or how you will be affected when you fail. In doing this you will automatically neutralize your affirmations.

Think of what blocks you have now. For example, if you do not have enough money, then affirm that 'money is a symbol of creative energy'. Write or say this over and over again. If you have always been stingy and careful with money, you need to spend more impulsively based on your intuition. If you follow your intuition, you will not go broke. It will create more prosperity, abundance, happiness and more energy in your life. Affirm 'I deserve to spend my money on things I desire.'

If you are not doing what you want in life to earn money, then imagine you are doing exactly what you want in your life. You have a fabulous career that is fun. You are doing what you feel you love to do and you are receiving tremendous amounts of money for it. You feel relaxed, creative and powerful. You follow your intuition from moment to moment and are richly rewarded for it. You are energized and doing exactly what you want to be doing. Affirm 'I am receiving plenty of money for doing exactly what I want to do.'

The more you follow your intuition and trust yourself and take risks to follow your inner guidance, the more money you will have. Affirm 'the universe is now paying me to do what I really love.'

Most of us stay in humdrum, boring jobs for all of our lives to earn a living. It takes guts to break out and do what you want and love to do. It is only fear and conditioning that keeps you there, so if you can change your self-image by affirmations there are no limitations.

When you achieve a goal, acknowledge yourself and give

yourself a pat on the back. Better still, give yourself a gift. I always give myself a gift of jewellery or something special. Often we achieve things that we have been desiring and visualizing, and we forget to even notice that we have succeeded. I always look after myself very well. Affirm 'I love and appreciate myself the way I am.'

To be fully in control of your life, you must understand the world, develop your creativity and intellect, and go beyond emotion. Being in control of your finances and body keeps you in balance.

The energy of affirmations for me has been in saying, 'I am moving forward, there are no limitations, I am moving up. I am going to live life to the full. Any opportunities that present themselves I will take. I will para-chute, I will fly an aeroplane, I will get my advanced certificate in scuba diving, I will have five children, I will have my own successful business, I will travel the world 100 times, I will visit every art gallery in the world, I will write three best-seller books, I will live in luxury for the rest of my life and travel first class all the way, I will scuba dive all over the world, I will make millions, I will have a fantastic relationship of uncon-ditional love, I will own the best art in the world, I will be happy and appreciative of my abundance and my life. This all happens in the first 45 years, then we start again!!'

Peace is the way – love is the answer

It is all out there waiting for you. You can do what you want; there are no limitations. I have completed the first part, now I cannot wait for the rest. Whoopee! Want to come along for the ride?

Some affirmations you may like to use

- ○ I express love to everyone I meet, for I know I am truly loveable.

- ○ Today I am joyful, successful and prosperous.

- ○ I am now creating my life the way I want it to be with no limitations.

- ○ I release the old and make way for the new.

- ○ I am willing and open to change.

- ○ As I follow my intuition, creative energy flows through me.

- ○ By being myself and doing what I love, I make a significant contribution to life.

- ○ I am a loving, passionate, beautiful person.

- ○ As I relax and let go, I flow towards my greatest good.

- ○ I am living in harmony with the universe.

- ○ Within me is a special place of serenity and power.

- ○ The universe is abundant. I feel abundant and all my needs are met.

- ○ I am healthy, wealthy and wise.

- ○ I feel successful, creative and strong and see beauty in all things.

- ○ I accept all people as they are and accept the world as it is. By becoming detached I reach a higher level of energy within me.

- ○ I love and accept myself the way I am.

- ○ I love and accept all people as they are.

For the ideal weight:

- ○ I deserve to maintain my perfect weight at 130lb, no matter what I eat.

- ○ It is okay to be perfect.

○ I refuse to punish myself by overeating.

○ I deserve to have a fantastic body.

○ I am ready to feel light and happy.

○ It is safe for me to give up my fat I used for protection.

○ I forgive myself for eating food when I wanted love.

○ I love myself and eat whatever I like without getting fat.

○ Everything I eat turns to health and beauty.

There is no limit to affirmations you can do to suit yourself and what you want to achieve. See yourself:

○ To be so centred that nothing can disturb your peace of mind.

○ To uplift and make all your friends feel they are important.

○ To be cheerful at all times and give everyone you meet a smile.

○ To give so much time to the improvement of yourself that you have no time to criticize and judge others.

○ To be optimistic and see the best in everyone and everything.

○ To talk health, wealth and happiness to every person you meet.

○ To be too big for worry, too strong for anger and fear and too happy to permit the presence of trouble.

• •

Help yourself

An affirmation is a positive thought that you consciously choose to immerse in your consciousness to achieve a desired result. Saying an affirmation or writing it is a way of loving yourself. As you start to change your way of thinking, you will feel a little strange at first, but if you keep making the affirmation, the resistance will be dissolved and the affirmation will eventually be integrated into your consciousness and the new thought will manifest. Think positive thoughts about your partner and loved ones. Holding on to negative thoughts about them only reinforces their negatives.

Do not spend time in the distractions of life. Try and spend as much time as possible moving towards your goal. Cut people short if they waste your time. Use your free time to the maximum: to study, to learn, to indulge in life, to understand and improve yourself. Use your experiences and mistakes to assist you in your next challenge. Move ahead with determination and drive.

Tie up all loose ends, complete and clear up misunderstandings in relationships, pay all your debts, clear out cupboards and make your life simple. Clear out all the clutter. Leave others alone and concentrate on yourself. This will allow the energy to flow and you will be in control in all circumstances. If you see something good, move towards it. If it is ugly, run away. Do not waste time on gossip. It takes too much energy. Cut out all distractions. Drop all the wimps and whiners out of your life. You can reach out to them, but if they do not want to be helped, leave them be. Your life is too important and you have too much to do to waste your time on them.

What you think, say and believe affects what you do, who you have a relationship with, how you feel and your health. They aren't just silly sayings, they are antidotes to all the negative thinking and garbage you have been feeding yourself all your life. Affirmations can open the door to good, happy and prosperous things coming your way.

Transforming the negative into positive

Every time you think negative thoughts about yourself or make yourself wrong, your emotional body changes its vibration and your energy drops. When the vibration becomes lower, your magnetism changes and you attract people and events that amplify this drop in energy. When you take responsibility and

In a few words ■ ■ ■ ■ ■ ■ ■ ■ ■ ■ ■ ■ ■

If you think you can, you can. If you think you cannot, then affirm that you can. What you believe you are, you are. What you believe you can do, you can achieve.

Accept yourself and your circumstances. Do not blame others. If you do not like your situation, change it. By concentrating on your own life, you become powerful and prosperous.

Above all, have laughter and fun. Do a few crazy things instead of living seriously and sanely, hour after hour, day after day, lighten up and leave 'em all laughing!

Affirmations create space for your reality to manifest itself. By changing what you say, you can change what you see and attract something you want into your life.

■ ■

attune your awareness to higher thoughts, creating joyful images in your mind, you can raise the vibration of your emotional body. If you find the people you know are constantly depressed or angry or in a negative emotional state, ask yourself what belief you have that says it is good for you to be in that environment.

Coming from a negative background and environment, I had developed habits and patterns in relationships that repeated themselves. When I released those patterns and focused on what was right in them, the areas that were giving me problems became resolved even though I was not trying to solve the problems. The more I focused on problems, the more relationships went downhill. But if I focused on them and held a high vision of them, the relationships improved.

You can transform the energy around a situation by seeing the good in people. When you point out the bad habits of others, the more insecure you make them feel, and from that base of insecurity you actually create and enlarge the problems you focus on. If you hear people complaining, stop them. If you listen to people moaning and listen to their negativity, you are putting yourself in a position of being affected by their lower energy. You do not need to listen. Refocus them on the positive and you will be doing the same for your own energy.

Do television, newspapers or the books you read use positive words? Do they bring up your energy or drain you and plant negative images in your mind? You are free to choose what you read and hear. No one makes you do anything. Most of the newspapers increase their circulation by transmitting negative news, events and negativity in people's lives.

Take responsibility for your life and fill yourself with love

The most important thing I found in releasing old patterns was to laugh at myself and not take myself too seriously. It is not the end of the world if something does not go right or the way I want it to. It is a learning experience. To be able to laugh at yourself and put your problems into perspective is a skill and releases negativity. It is very funny to see ourselves in situations and wonder why and how we put ourselves there, but learn from the experience.

You cannot leave the past and old patterns until you love them. The more you hate something or someone you are bound to the event or them. The more you love your past; you are free from it. When you can think of your parents and childhood and know that they were perfect for the path you are on, you are free from the effects of the past. When you change your negative memories into positive understanding, you can go even faster into your new future.

When you decide to take responsibility for your own life, you can look at your past experiences and understand the reasons you chose those life events to strengthen you. Keeping old memories of guilt and sadness alive in your cells does damage to your physical body. When you realize that you created these experiences to grow but can now choose to remember these events with love, you can heal your body and your mind. Release the old memories and fill yourself with love.

Meditation to release old memories and fill yourself with love

Meditate and visualize yourself in your childhood.

○ What are you doing, what do you feel? See your family and remember what happened at school. Imagine you are playing an old movie of your life and actually feel what happened.

○ Acknowledge your feelings of fear, sadness, loss or whatever they were, but recognize what you learnt from that experience and then see it with love and compassion.

○ And the people who were with you, what were they teaching you? See each experience with your teachers, family and loved ones and express gratitude and love. This transforms the negative thought-forms and opens your creativity; you feel lighter and more at peace with yourself and can tune in to a frequency of love and harmony.

○ As you increase your love vibration by clearing your body of negative thought forms and emotions that block love, you enter a higher dimension, a finer frequency vibration of love, peace and harmony, and become unlimited.

Chapter 11

Creating special relationships

Relationships do not just happen. We create them with conscious effort and work. Love requires an awareness of what is required to make your loved ones and yourself happy and fulfilled. It requires honesty about what you truly feel and genuinely wish to give.

Relationships are not determined by fate or luck, but are the result of ongoing decisions for which each partner is responsible. Your actions can make, break or bond the relationship. You have the choice to become lazy or keep the love alive. The course of love is in your hands and is about acceptance, not change.

As you know, love is the greatest healer. Whenever you love, you experience an opportunity to grow, to expand your level of vitality and to become whole. Every relationship offers a unique and powerful opportunity to heal yourself if you are willing to take advantage of it.

Nothing approaches love in its ability to purify. If you want to be pure, find someone you love and let him, or her, love you. After I left my first husband I was very hurt and my self-esteem was very low. Not until I married again and surrendered to loving and being loved fully, did I ever experience the purity of my own essence.

Love alone is the ultimate purification process because love alone is absolutely pure. It cannot tolerate impurity, sickness, negativity of any kind, and brings up anything unlike itself for the purpose of release. When you are in love, you are in a state of deep gratitude for all of creation. The feeling of utter perfection in your heart opens your eyes to all that God has given you.

When you surrender to love, you emerge from behind your ego and experience your oneness and completeness. You are able to receive total bliss, joy and an at-one feeling with another being. Looking into the eyes of someone you love, perceiving the beauty of that person's spirit is like looking into the mirror of your own soul.

My commitment in a relationship is to truth, honesty and intimacy. To anyone I love I promise to do the best I can, to tell the truth, to be vulnerable and to share my feelings, to take responsibility for myself, to honour the connection I feel with that person, and to maintain that connection, no matter how the form may change. I promise to totally accept the other person and myself and to love them unconditionally and not to try and change them.

Real commitment makes no guarantees about a relationship's form; real commitment allows for the fact that form is constantly changing and that we can trust that process of change. It opens the door to the true intimacy that is created when people share deeply and honestly with one another. If two people stay together on this basis, it is because they really want to be together. They continue to find an intensity of love and learning with each other as they change and grow.

The importance of self-worth

Most people are not true to themselves and are living a lie so how can they be true to their mates? They are playing a game, wearing a mask and presenting an image of what they think their mate wants to see. While most of us have learnt to wear masks for survival, it takes quite a lot of energy as we are not being true to ourselves, and not being totally honest to how we feel. When you do this, you sell your integrity and your energy level depletes. When you can be totally honest, drop the mask and reveal your true self – warts, flaws and all nerdy qualities – it frees up tremendous amounts of energy. If you are always pretending to be something you are not, it places stress on you. When you cannot live up to the image, it presents problems and conflict. As a result, when you do actually experience true love, all your fears and patterns from the past can get activated. The result is that you want love and intimacy and at the same time you fear it and unconsciously defend yourself against it. All love and healing is release from fear.

With self-acceptance comes the courage to risk being intimate

You may fear abandonment and feel it is safer not to reveal your true self. You may feel it is safer not to get too close or care too much, when your partner may leave you anyhow. Love may not last, couples do break up and you may have decided that nothing lasts forever. This is based on fear, and the idea that what you resist persists. But usually this very fear brings about the abandonment you are so afraid of. People who are too guarded, who fear intimacy, who choose to insulate themselves from the normal risks involved in loving openly, often set in motion a process of turning away and finally face rejection, the very thing they wanted so desperately to avoid.

Loss is painful, and if you do lose someone you usually forget how nourishing the love was, you only remember the pain of the loss. You create your own dramas but, except for early childhood experiences, it is you who is responsible for the quality and direction of your relationships. You do not have to be the victim of your experiences; you are the writer, producer, director and star of them. All of us are hurt at some time in our lives, we cannot prevent ourselves from being hurt, but you can reduce the probability of being hurt in the same way again if you change your patterns. Change is frightening, but it is also a chance to grow and an empowering adventure to experience a new way of being. We often believe that we cannot break self-defeating patterns, or do not want to. If you resist and insist on not changing and act with rigidity or fear, you create the same circumstances again and again, until you finally learn and change, if you ever do.

If you have doubts about your own self-worth, and feel you are bad or unacceptable, you may feel that your lover will judge you in the way you judge yourself. Revealing your true self means offering yourself up for critical judgement, and you feel that if your true self emerges, he or she will not like you.

When you are in a deeply caring relationship, it does mean you take the risk of rejection, abandonment and loss. Love and self-acceptance give the courage to risk being intimate, and by doing so you reap the reward of a fulfilling relationship. As you have courage to shed your layers of protective defences, and stop trying to pretend you are 'perfect', you find your partner will be drawn even closer. If you share sad, embarrassing and awkward moments, you experience intense closeness. When you risk a fuller expression of yourself, face the fears you have about being your true self and being known – fears of embarrassment, false pride and letting your flaws show – you find that people accept you as you truly are. This frees you from feeling compelled to be perfect to avoid being seen as defective and not enough. By exposing your true self you feel more alive and by not wearing the mask of perfection, attract intimacy.

Love and happiness cannot be found in another person whom you think will fulfil your lack or needs, or in money, possessions, drugs, fame or glory, food or beautiful clothes, as all the advertising tells us constantly that we need in order to be attractive and loveable. It can only be found inside. It is not that any of these things are necessarily wrong or bad, they are simply not the source, and what we long for is the experience of our complete connection to the source. We have an infinite supply of love within us. We think that we have to get something from outside in order to be happy, but we must learn to contact the inner source of happiness and flow it outward to share with others.

Creating a positive relationship

Mates are not the solution to erasing past experiences and hurts that have led to feelings of inadequacy and low self-esteem. A loving relationship should be devoted to the purpose of having fun and becoming all you can be and seeing the divine essence in your partner and yourself. This kind of relationship is possible, so why settle for anything less.

Many relationships are based on the dynamics of co-dependency or need-obligate, and sacrifice and manipulation through guilt. Within it, partners feel they cannot share themselves completely and tend to withhold from each other, afraid to tell each other the complete truth. It ultimately seems to diminish its participants. It leaves them feeling less alive and passionate and more guilty and afraid. They end up rationalizing their feelings of separation, settling for less than they really want, and getting to be right about how unsatisfying life or relationships can be.

A poor relationship is based on differences, where each one thinks the other has what he has not. They come together to complete themselves by robbing the other and stay until they think there is nothing left to steal, and then move on. A loving relationship starts from each one looking within and seeing no lack. Accepting your completion, you would extend it by joining

In a few words ■ ■ ■ ■ ■ ■ ■ ■ ■ ■ ■ ■ ■

The people you are in relationships with are always mirrors reflecting your beliefs – and you are a mirror, reflecting their beliefs. So a relationship is one of the most powerful tools for growth that you have.

Take total responsibility for your relationship and assume that you alone are responsible for creating it the way it is. If there are things you do not like, try to detach yourself and ask yourself why you have created it this way and what beliefs you have that cause you to create a less than satisfying or unhappy relationship.

If you really desire to have a happy, joyful and deeply fulfilling relationship, believe it is possible and are willing to accept that happiness, then you can and will create the perfect partner for you.

■ ■

with another, whole as yourself. If you want the 'perfect' relationship, start with your relationship with yourself. In a way, you could say that there is only one real relationship going on for any of us. It is the relationship inside of us, the relationship between the spirit and the body.

We are all looking for unconditional, uncritical, non-judgmental love. But you will not find it outside yourself until you find it inside yourself. You are completely filled with love and your supply is limitless. When you give your love unconditionally to others with no expectations of return, the love within extends, expands and joins. By giving love away you increase the love within and everyone around gains and is happy. You have everything you need now and the essence of your being is love. Letting go of the great search for the perfect love and looking within for your own reservoir of love will free up tremendous amounts of energy. Give your love with no conditions or expectations. The giving leads to a sense of inner peace and joy that is unrelated to time. To give love you must love and accept yourself first and that is the hardest thing for most of us. We constantly judge ourselves and find fault with ourselves. Out of the billions of people on the earth, there are many that are lonely because they put up walls and will not let in the love.

In the search for love we are really searching for completion. Most of us feel incomplete, which comes from the fear of being alone. We try and get this from outside ourselves, from another person. But because we want to get rather than to give, we clash with the person we hope will gratify these wishes.

The experiences of childhood

For those of you fortunate enough to have loving parents who cared for you and gave positive confirmation about yourself, you will have learnt to incorporate your parents' love and their ability to comfort you. In perceiving yourself through their eyes, you will have learnt to give yourself self-love. You will have learnt to be less anxious and complete in yourself, and will have developed a strong sense of self, which now enables you to deal with life very effectively.

Unfortunately, most of us had parents who were flawed, neglectful and inconsistent in their love, which resulted in a sense of 'lack' and underdevelopment. In turn, this resulted in an inability to comfort ourselves, which may resort in seeking external sources of comfort; in other people, food, drugs, alcohol, continuous shopping, or trying to get love; any intense outside stimulus that will block the pain of self-doubt and incompleteness.

When parenting is incomplete, there is a feeling that if we could merge with another person we would achieve that wonderful safe and secure feeling we felt with our mother. We lust for someone who will give us the love we do not feel for ourselves, someone who will make us feel whole.

Another need is to feel good about ourselves, to have self-esteem. We feel unworthy and have low self-esteem because of our childhood experiences of disapproval. We continuously need to seek external proof of our value or that we are loved if we did not receive this as a child. If our parents encouraged us to think for ourselves and through our experiences came to value ourselves, we would have our own approval and would not continuously need to seek it from others, and look to others to tell us and confirm that we are okay. As adults who have not learnt to validate themselves we remain forever searching for the person who will make us feel good enough and acceptable.

We also search for love in order to feel alive, recharge our batteries and feel excited about life. If you failed to receive physical contact, warmth and closeness as a child, you would feel empty and sad as an adult and constantly seek outside stimulation. You may seek sex to feel stimulated, vibrant and flowing, or through drinking, drugs or eating you can feel a temporary sense of well being.

We grow up trying to compensate for all the things we were missing in childhood. Once you understand and are aware of your incompleteness, you can learn to love and be loved, and avoid any unrealistic expectations of Prince or Princess Charming to make up for all of your inadequacies. When you do not expect someone else to complete you, you will drop the blaming, resenting and the disappointment, which stems from your expectations and avoid the disillusionment that happens in your relationships.

Moving to unconditional love

Once you accept your separateness, even though you want to love and be loved and develop a strong sense of self, you will be able to love another person successfully. Your own self-worth comes from your own estimation of yourself; it is not something that someone else can give you. Mature love is an appreciation of someone for who they are rather than what you would like that person to be or to give you. Pure unconditional and unselfish love goes beyond your own needs and concerns and exists when another person's security and satisfaction are as important to you as your own.

Understanding and accepting your partner creates power, because you can let go completely to a person you feel safe and trust, being known and still valued for the true you. If you can understand and accept and love people for who they truly are, with all their inadequacies and rough edges and flaws, you will have a magnetism that draws people to you. It is easy to love someone at his or her best, but the hardest challenge is to love them at their worst. We are all aware of inadequacies and irritating aspects of our mates, but we lovingly accept them without building resentment or blame. To truly accept another person you must first accept yourself, and give up being overly critical and judgmental. If you are critical with yourself, you will also be that way with your mate. Unconditional love demands a maturity that means being able to care while at the same time perceiving both the good and the bad. You can tell a person when they do something that upsets you, but you love, forgive and accept them anyway. When you love them in spite of their flaws, they will want to work harder to be the best they can be and they will love you more for your acceptance of them.

Accepting small flaws, especially if they are outweighed by qualities you like and respect, will provide the comfort, security and freedom the other person so craves and desires. Most of us know we have weaknesses and inadequacies. If your mate accepts and loves you any way, it gives you a boost and confidence to face the world and you will love them more for them giving it to you. To totally accept a person for who and what they are with no expectations of anything in return is true unconditional love. Accepting their vulnerabilities and revealing yours to them lets people in and makes you closer. To feel understood, accepted and trusted gives a fulfilling and intimate relationship.

You continually attract people to you that are like you, so if you are looking for the perfect partner with particular characteristics you must first have those characteristics to attract that person with the same vibration. Like attracts like. If you want unconditional love you must first be able to give it.

Use visual imagery in meditation to change your negative beliefs and visualize creating beautiful, loving, fulfilling and joyful relationships. Surround yourself and your loved ones with energy and gold light and look at them and say, 'You are what you are and I love you unconditionally.' See them smile at you with love and joy and know you are centred in love and acceptance of all those around you.

In a few words ■■■■■■■■■■■■■

When you can feel concern for another person and have empathy with them, you experience true love, which is loving, understanding and accepting people as they are. Only when you have a strong sense of self are you able to love in this way.

When you are willing to move from your own selfish wishes and needs and emotional intensity to giving total acceptance and unconditional love, you commit to a more spiritual path.

In order to commit to another requires the courage to love, and the willingness to risk, to be so secure in yourself that you can trust.

There are no guarantees in love, but you choose to commit and give it, no matter what happens. The truth is that love is limitless and you have so much to give.

■■■■■■■■■■■■■■■■■■■■■■■■■■

Nurture yourself

It is important to take time for yourself – when you are balanced and centred, all around you works smoothly. Take responsibility for yourself first and let others take responsibility for themselves. Mothers especially fall into the trap of doing everything for others in the family and neglecting themselves. It does not pay to be a martyr. By not looking after your needs first, you become resentful, tired and worn out and your energy levels get low and you become bad tempered and cannot cope with life. You become depressed and miserable and send out negative energy that people do not like to be around. It is not selfish to look after yourself and your needs first; it is for the benefit of all the family that you are centred, balanced and happy.

Have a love affair with yourself. Do not wait for your partner to make you happy. You create your own reality and by making yourself happy and taking responsibility for your own happiness, you do not have to blame him or her when you feel miserable. Draw guidelines so everyone is clear what you will do and what you will not. It is up to you to create the scene and then others will fall into place. To give love you must love and take care of yourself first. Loving yourself does not take away from loving others; love multiplies and expands and comes back to you. You can give yourself security, pleasure and approval and come from a centred place inside.

Letting go of negative beliefs about yourself and all the limiting beliefs and thoughts you have been hiding behind is essential. To have pure love of oneself, or unconditional acceptance and respect for yourself under all circumstances, can seem like a big sacrifice. In order to forgive yourself completely and surrender to your own true essence, you must give up all the lies, all the limiting thoughts you have been hiding behind and realize your own magnificence, letting go of who you pretend to be and fear you might be. The truth is that you are good enough just the way you are; you are perfect and worthy of God's love and you are already loved. Once you get your mind out of the way, pure love is all that remains. When you choose to love everyone unconditionally, you accelerate the process of loving yourself unconditionally, since everyone you love is a reflection of yourself.

If you can love one person totally and completely and hold no grievances, you can forgive everyone. If you can love one person totally and completely, you can love everyone. Respect each other, be best friends, show appreciation and do not blame others, have fun together and take time to share and to have pleasure together. Give unconditional love without hooks. But to have the perfect relationship you must love yourself first. Relationships are not outside, they are inside you. As you learn to love yourself, you automatically receive the love and appreciation from others that you desire.

> Take responsibility for yourself and let others take responsibility for themselves

Marriage creates the perfect scene to blame another for our inadequacies. When you are living on your own you can only blame yourself for your unhappiness, but if you are married and unhappy, it is because of you! It is easier to blame your partner and hold him or her responsible for your unhappiness and misery than to take the responsibility for yourself. The more responsibility you take for what you want, the less you need to blame others, and the happier you become.

I am often asked, since I have been on the spiritual and emotional quest and attended various seminars, whether I think it is important to have your partner or husband go with you. Many people, especially wives, think it is essential to have their husbands do what they do and worry if they do not; maybe they will change and their husbands won't. The truth is that you do not have to control your husband or partner into doing what you do. You must give each other space to develop in the areas each wants to, whether it is in this area or learning to play tennis or scuba dive. You do not have to be with each other continuously. If you are in contact with your own source of love, it will not matter if your mate is pursuing the same path or not. You will find that spiritual energy in that person will pull you together.

Relationships and sex

Many of us find sex such a serious subject and have certain fears around it. Fear of sex comes from belief structures that say that sex is evil and taboo. The Catholic Church does not accept birth control; sex is not for enjoyment! The way we are not told anything means that we grow up not knowing what happens. Very few of us had parents that sat us down and lovingly explained what it was all about. We learnt from other children or were told that 'babies come from under a cabbage leaf'. We lived in fear of being found out if we experimented and explored our bodies by playing 'doctors'.

There are fears around expectations, disease – AIDS and other sexually-transmitted diseases – fear of pregnancy, fear of failure, loss of power, commitment, impotency, inhibitions, intimacy, imperfections, rejection and inadequacy. The more sex you have, the more you want. The less you have, the less you want. When you give up the fear, which goes with the excitement, you allow yourself to see sex without the tension. You can have sex and laughter and get rid of the tension, stress and pain around sex. When you give up fear, you get real intimacy, tenderness, consciousness, communication and warmth.

However, sex can be a substitute for intimacy. You can pry the other person's eye open and say, 'Hi!' Actually look at who you are making love to. How many of you do not even dare to open your eyes when you have sex? Look at each other and enjoy. Lighten up and have fun with sex. It can be discussed. Like a dinner date, you can giggle a lot and decide where to have sex and who should go on top! Make an appointment for sex. We make an appointment for everything else, like a business

In a few words ■ ■ ■ ■ ■ ■ ■ ■ ■ ■ ■ ■ ■ ■ ■

Every being was born spiritual and you can choose to focus on that or not.

Love and being centred will affect your partner; when you change and improve yourself you will find that your partner changes as well.

When you give up the various power games that you have been playing with each other, your partner will have no one to play with. You will then both have more energy, more connection, and come together energetically with the magnetic pull of honesty and love.

You are central to the purpose of your life, not your partner, and your own personal growth is your responsibility alone.

■ ■

appointment or a lunch date. So why is sex less important that it should not be put on the calendar?

Do not be so serious. Share embarrassing sexual moments. By sharing they can be very connecting. Role reverse. Chase each other around the room and laugh. Sex can be fun. Do not laugh while pointing though, that may spoil the whole relationship! Laugh with, not laugh at.

Most of us are overly preoccupied with work and feel stressed and need a balance. Playing and having fun and experiencing the vitality of a good relationship is important. Do not be afraid to create a little suspense and intrigue. A little distance is good for a relationship. If you want to do something by yourself, do not feel guilty. When you take care of your own desires and needs, you stimulate romance by not being available all the time. By doing new and exciting things, you do not let the relationship stagnate.

Being alive is being and showing more of yourself. If you need to be accepted and approved of, things are usually hidden that you feel others would not like about you and you expose only the good things. But by allowing yourself to be vulnerable, you are trusting and assuming that you are worth being loved for what you are. We all have fears and doubts about our sexual desirability. We feel inhibited and self-conscious because we feel we are not good enough, attractive enough and loveable. Learning to be less inhibited and more passionate and expressive risks appearing foolish. When you allow yourself to take that risk, you will feel more powerful and alive. When you are at ease with yourself and let your feelings emerge spontaneously, you

In a few words ■■■■■■■■■■■■■■

Mae West was the biggest sex queen of all time. She made sex light. She brought laughter to sex. She said things like, 'When I'm good I'm very, very good; when I'm bad I'm better!' 'Too much of a good thing is wonderful.' 'Is that a banana in your pocket, or are you happy to see me?'

The same can't be said of Marilyn Monroe. She was sultry, passionate and could never say no. How society has gone down the drain for us to worship this poor girl, who came from a background of incest and unhappiness and was taken advantage of by so many people in high places. She eventually found life unbearable and committed suicide. Or did she? We are still left wondering if she was murdered.

Then there is Doris Day, who represents the girl next door who does things for men but who never leads her own life and must have the guy in the end or evaporate off the screen. She comes across as being desperate for approval.

■■■■■■■■■■■■■■■■■■■■■■■■■■■

arouse passion and desire in your partner.

You do not start out being passionate; it becomes part of you if you want it. If you want to be sexy you may feel self-conscious, as you would do if you were learning to play tennis or swim for the first time. Once you overcome awkwardness you become more natural and comfortable with feeling sexy and passionate.

If you have trouble releasing feelings and allowing yourself to be more passionate, use visualization. You cannot do anything unless you can visualize yourself doing it, and this includes becoming less inhibited. In your meditation, imagine yourself acting in a more passionate and sexy way. Picture yourself saying and doing things that are carefree and uninhibited. By imagining and visualizing yourself being less restrained you will open up the way for you to be this way with your partner. When you can arouse passion and desire in your partner, he or she will feel stimulated and attracted to you, more intimate, loving, romantic and comfortable, and this will form a close bond.

So lighten up around sex; enjoy each other and take responsibility for yourself. When you make an appointment for sex, it gives you time to think about it. Should you use precautions, does your partner have any diseases? Do you even want to do it with that particular partner? Stop and think. You do not have to lose control and rush into a sexual encounter without considering the consequences.

Giving and receiving

Because most of us fear expression of our emotions, sex is used as a way to get closer. Passion and lust is used as a way of contact and getting close. Boys especially are taught to hide their emotions in order to maintain self-control, and to express and open up raises the fear of shame and embarrassment. But fears that are repressed become damaging and toxic. Once you can overcome this fear and risk opening up you move on to a much more intimate relationship, one which includes feeling comfortable, feeling accepted and so trust and friendship develops.

You may fear that the development of real friendship in the relationship may lead to loss of excitement and passion, but this is not true, lovers can be friends. Passion is only lost because of an accumulation of hurt and resentment. When you can remain friends and communicate your feelings, you can release blame and resentment from the relationship. Lovers who are intimate friends share the mutual acceptance and openness that leads them to want to make love, and have something to share and talk about after making love. When you can feel relaxed, open and trusting, you will feel more companionship and want to be with your partner more. Partners who play together, stay together, and form a powerful and fulfilling bond.

Maintaining the desire for sex in a relationship does not just happen. Despite the best intentions, relationships are often taken for granted. It is easy to become lazy and less sensitive to our partner. To keep a good relationship, you have to continually maintain and give to it. Be responsible for your actions and realize that love requires an awareness of what is needed to make your loved one happy and fulfilled. By continuing to nurture that love, it will not only survive, but also escalate and grow and have an ongoing quality of vitality and warmth.

Love rarely dies; negative feelings, resentment and blame only mask it. Everyone makes mistakes and hurts or disappoints us sometimes. But you have the choice to forgive and go on or to accumulate resentment. Forgiving unlocks love. It does not matter how angry or hurt you may be, to blame and punish will kill love; you cannot love in a positive way until you choose to forgive and let go of painful negative feelings. This is the only way for the relationship to move on to a more intimate, warm and loving partnership. By choosing to hold on to blame and resentment and punishing your mate (even a look can kill), you block the energy of love, remain dormant and love gradually dies. Learn to love without possessiveness. Realize that those things or people you love are as individual as you are, and they have the right to their own individuality.

Do not assume that your mate knows what you desire, your wishes or what hurts you. When you take responsibility for your own life, you are also responsible for making yourself known to those you love. If you do not communicate, you are setting yourself up to be a victim. When you tell your partner what you need and he or she responds to it, it is a real indication of their love for you. You do not have to think that if you have to tell your mate what you need, they do not love you. They are not a mind reader, but a mate who cares enough to listen and respond lovingly is worth a million.

Unconditional love requires complete unselfishness and giving, but giving is contagious, and is generally returned in abundance. Giving only to receive is not love, but if you find yourself continually giving with nothing in return maybe you should find another partner, one who deserves your love. Feeling good about yourself leads to feeling confident about yourself, which makes love happen and keeps it alive.

To attract a partner, most of us think we need a fantastic physical body. This is not so. It may attract a partner initially, but a person's attitude, behaviour, personality and emotional response are more powerful in attracting and bonding than what is on the outside. When you can develop a warm, comfortable feeling of friendship, you develop a warm, intimate relationship that can only get better and better and when you are with someone who totally accepts you and loves you any way, why would you ever feel the need to leave.

The blissful state of good sex

Sex is a matter of energy. The more energy you have, the more blissful you can be, and the better sex becomes. Orgasm is an energy event that can be learned outside and duplicated independent of the sexual context. The true source of your pleasure lies not in your partner but within yourself and when you realize this you can feel empowered to take responsibility for your own well-being in sex. As the energy between your bodies melts and merges, sexual communion becomes an experience of deep intimacy. When lovemaking is gentle and slow, you can transform the energy of sexual arousal into an experience of pure bliss.

Visualize your perfect partner

Most lovemaking is vigorous and dynamic; you breathe hard, building up sexual passion until you explode the energy outward in a final release. In Tantric lovemaking, you slowly and gently enter effortlessly into a sense of floating, as if your body is expanding to an orgasm of the brain. This fusion creates the experience of ecstasy in which body, mind, heart and spirit all participate.

Our culture has mostly lost the understanding that sexual energy is a physical expression of spiritual power. The desire to unite sexually with another person is a reflection of an underlying spiritual need to experience wholeness and complete intimacy, to transcend the sense of separateness and isolation. It is a need to return to the original source of creation, to the oneness within the self. Sexual union, which is carried out only for the sake of pleasure, rarely satisfies our needs completely. But with the sacred element added you can experience a connection between the life force itself and your deepest creative impulses.

Sex is often misused as it is associated with personal power, conquest or dominance, and when it is a purely physical, instinctual drive that is not held in reverence, sexual energy is repressed and eventually directed against life itself, which results in disrespect, abuse, disease and other forms of sexual violence. Negative social conditioning about sex creates fear, which blocks spontaneity, pleasure and an ability to love, honour and respect one another and be truly intimate.

Beliefs can also limit sexual potential. We all naturally have within us the potential to experience wholeness and fulfilment in our love lives. Unfortunately, this has been often clouded over by beliefs that sex is shameful, sex is only for procreation, etc. These wrong attitudes stop you from trusting yourself and discovering your own uniqueness. They prevent you from realizing that sex can be expanded to embrace the body, mind, heart and spirit, instead of just experiencing hard, aggressive and fast intercourse. The preparation for love-making is not just physical stimulation, but a delicate harmonization between lovers that requires openness, trust, creativity, emotional and spiritual qualities.

The belief that you are dependent on a partner who is responsible for your sexual fulfilment is based on the assumption that the source of your pleasure is not within you, but a result of what is done to you and how it is done to you by your lover. When you can accept that you are responsible for your own sexual pleasure, you can experience ecstasy.

Everything that a person experiences, whether you may judge it as good or bad, is an opportunity for learning. Every situation is an opportunity to become more aware about who you are and how you can expand your capacities, to embrace wholeness. Within each of us is a natural, unspoiled, childlike spirit who can openly and innocently explore. The innocence of this spirit remains intact and is our natural capacity to enjoy life, to play, to love and to be ecstatic, energizing and life-giving.

You are important in a sexual relationship

Loving yourself, the ability to trust yourself and listen to your inner voice, the intuitive guidance of your own heart, makes you aware that you deserve the experience of ecstasy and are not willing to compromise or settle for less than that. Trying to love another when you do not love yourself does not work, you usually feel possessive, dependent or jealous. When you really begin to love yourself, you become a magnet, attracting the love of others. You do not need the others to feel whole; love becomes a state of being. When you feel abundant, you want to share and celebrate, to give and receive. This is a true free partnership and you will experience the sexual loving that is a delicate co-creation between two equal partners, honouring each other's differences, but moving beyond them into a space of respect and devotion. When you make a conscious choice to surrender to your partner, to open your heart and trust, you give yourself voluntarily to the highest aspect of your potential so you can grow and become complete.

When you enter into a loving relationship with yourself, which does not mean being self-absorbed or narcissistic or disregarding others, you become both the lover, the one who gives love, and the beloved, the one who receives it. Through this self-directed love, you can experience yourself as a limitless being, in tune with the whole of existence. The more accepting of yourself you are, the more your energy is unified. When you criticize yourself, one part of you is fighting another part, and your energy is in conflict. Orgasm requires your total participation, and when your energy is fully unified, you can enjoy pleasure and become fully orgasmic in love and move towards the source of your own being.

If you have a deep-seated fear within yourself, which makes you resist or hold back, try to understand where it comes from. Discuss it with your partner and feel it. Part of your growth process is to move through fear and when you can, you will experience a release of blocked energy, followed by enhanced pleasure. Knowledge of fear is a good teacher of where your blocked energy is.

When you can stay in the present moment, to allow yourself to be fully engaged in what you are doing, and maintain that attitude, without thinking about what you have to do next, without worrying or comparing, that is when you will experience sexual ecstasy.

Meditation can help you appreciate the concept of being present in each moment, living in the 'now'. Sexual ecstasy happens when you are so completely absorbed by the fullness of the present moment that nothing else exists. The present is the only real moment, the only reality that you can feel, experience and learn from. Loving and feeling good about yourself and focusing on what does work in your life is an approach that assumes you are already whole and healthy and naturally capable of great enjoyment. This may require a shift in perspective and encouragement for you to realize you can have and deserve unlimited pleasure.

If you feel imperfect or inadequate, use visualization to create pictures in your mind to learn to love and appreciate yourself. Close your eyes and imagine a time in your past when you felt totally loved, cared for and protected. You may remember being a child in your mother's arms. Feel how it felt – secure, gentle – and imagine how you felt – open and trusting. By cultivating your awareness of various feelings of love and trust, you have an opportunity to expand the joy in your life and break the habit of focusing on problems rather than pleasure.

The symbol of yin and yang represents the continuity of the life force, which is movement. It is the symbols of the complementary principles of negative and positive, receptive and active, female and male. Yin as the receptive, feminine, and yang as the creative, masculine, complement each other. Though opposite, they are not in opposition or antagonistic; though different, they supplement each other in the continuous movement between them, without beginning and without end. When yang reaches its final movement, then yin is created and starts. This interplay of the two fundamental and vital elements implies perpetual motion; where their relationship in yin and yang is so perfect, they constitute equilibrium and harmony. The symbol indicates that which is held in balance yet separated. There is nothing without its opposite, nothing that does not change or move, in order to be permanent, to live, which in itself is a yin-yang statement. The yin-yang symbol was designed during the Sung Dynasty (960-1279AD) and has remained in all classics of Chinese literature.

In a few words ■■■■■■■■■■■■■■

Our deepest desire is intimacy and empathy, to feel safe enough with someone to show our sadness, hurt and vulnerabilities knowing that the response will be warmth and kindness rather than criticism and judgement. Our desire is to be totally accepted and loved for who and what we are. When you can be open, trusting and vulnerable and communicate how you feel, you will then feel a heart-to-heart connection with each other.

When your heart is flooded with love, there is no space for doubt, fear, lack or hurt. When you can love so completely that you have forgotten to ask yourself if you are loved in return, there is no 'lack'.

Expand the sensuality and vitality you get from your lover to your family, work and environment by including self-love, pleasure, relaxation and spontaneity in your life. By opening your heart, becoming more intimate and honest, you affect people who are close to you, your family, friends and workmates.

Creative freedom in love emerges when a balance is reached between the female and male, yielding and initiating roles. It is not only giving that brings pleasure, it is also receiving.

■■■■■■■■■■■■■■■■■■■■■■■■■■

Chapter 12

Creating
prosperity

People are as happy as they decide to be and people are about as prosperous as they decide to be. Developing a life of abundance is the result of deliberate decisions. People have traditionally blocked their prosperity-consciousness with decisions, which lead to self-defeating attitudes about money, self, power and love. You must first decide if it is okay for you to prosper. Fear of success has sometimes been called the fear of the sublime – the fear of acknowledging that we really are great and wonderful beings. That idea is more than many of us can stand. Being prosperous comes too close to proving it is true. It is hard to imagine that we do not necessarily desire success with all our heart and will, and yet, fear of success and poor self-image may be the greatest barriers we face.

Many people feel uncomfortable discussing money. Why? Because they have a belief structure or conditioning that says that money will not buy happiness, or that rich people are cruel and evil. The facts are that poor people are cruel and evil, too. The way we often judge others and ourselves is through money. How much we make, how we make it and spend it is a prime indicator of success. If you have the skills to survive in the corporate world, you are a 'winner'. This is our market value. Income is really our market value. Money is an exchange of energy and the more income you make the greater the public's appreciation of a job well done. Money brings power. Not power in itself, but how it will be spent gives power. The more money we have the more potential power we have.

Many people have the belief that 'Money is the root of all evil.' The actual statement in the New Testament is that 'The love of money is the root of all evil.' But if you are working with the energy of love to use the money for unselfish needs, to aid the world in the coming needs of reconstruction, not with the energy of desire, the reflection or distortion of love, the freer will be the inflow of that money which is needed to carry out the work. This requires spiritual energy, sound business sense, skill and financial support.

Prospering people are powerful. They have made friends with their personal power. They did not become strong; they acknowledged the strength they already had. Personal power comes from within and depends on you approving of yourself. It demands a total honesty that you need to be who you are without pretence and act on what you honestly feel.

Many people think finance is complicated, usually because they have never been educated about money matters. They also think you must be wealthy to invest, which is a myth. The first step is to make a commitment to yourself and to the future. You must set your goals and achieve them.

The principles for prosperity

1. The prosperity principle

Everything happens for our benefit: problems are our opportunity to grow. We cannot fail. We can choose not to go any further on a particular path. See the success of choosing to let go of what is not working. Money is the energy of divinity, and to fulfil our needs, we must work with the energy of love and not desire.

2. The scarcity principle

Never enough in life – money, sex, love. Many people feel inadequate in themselves. They feel incomplete and want something from others, but do not know exactly what. They love in order to receive. Love becomes a bartering point. When you demand love and money, the supply dries up. If you shut down your love vibration, with only conditional love for everyone, you put a restriction on your visible supply. Without love, there cannot be the full and complete manifestation and attraction of supply-in-form. The only thing you have is self-doubt. You resist change: 'the devil you know is better than the one you don't!' This keeps you in jobs, marriages and relationships you have outgrown but fear letting go of. Life is not to be enjoyed now, but saved up for the future.

Making your choice

The powerful and prosperous person has a choice. Based on your dreams and realistic evaluation of yourself and your environment, choose to live and let live. Cooperate, assist where you can and release when you cannot. Focus on what is possible instead of what is not. Money is a symbol of creative energy and profit is the expression to the public of a job well done. The more willing you are to open up to the universe, the more money you will have in your life. Your ability to earn and spend money abundantly and wisely is based on your ability to be a channel for the universe. The stronger and more open your channel is, the more money will flow through it. Do not hoard money. When you keep it moving it makes room for more money to flow back to you.

Be willing to take some risks with money and work. Listen to the intuitive voice that tells you to try something new, to be more creative or to move on to the next step on your path. If you cling on to what you think you should do to make money and be secure, and if you are not happy doing it, it will block the energy and make you feel tired and stressed. If you are using your creative energy and doing what you like to do, it will feel effortless. If you have always saved money and been very careful about spending it, you need to learn to spend more impulsively based on your intuition. If you want something, buy it. You deserve it. If you follow your intuition, you will not end up bankrupt; it will create more prosperity, abundance and enjoyment in your life and keep the money moving.

Earning a good salary, even a terrific salary, will never make you rich or even financially secure. To be those things you have to save money from your salary, fees, commissions or business, year after year, and invest it. If you start early enough, you can be in good financial shape well before retirement.

I can hear you say that yours is not a money brain; your eyes glaze at the mere mention of figures. You might as well say you don't understand dentistry and refuse to brush your teeth! Perhaps you dream that a rich relative or lover will dump a pile of money on you some day or you will win the lottery. It rarely happens. Most rich people have worked hard for their money or if they have inherited it they can be quite chintzy about handing out money to 'deserving waifs'. That is one reason they are rich! Even if they did, it would slip right through the fingers of someone with the wrong attitude towards money. People often say I am lucky, but it is extraordinary that the harder I work and the more I give, the luckier I seem to get.

To avoid being an old destitute some day, or even a middle-aged one and, assuming there is no genius in your life to manage your money, then you are probably going to have to make, save and invest money in order to be comfortable in your old age.

Saving your money

How do you save? Simple. Every pay-day, march to the bank or your financial adviser and deposit something, no matter how small. It sounds easy. Anybody can do it, but it takes guts and particular determination. You have to be cheap in the early years and careful about waste. It is never too late to start being thrifty, and you must. Do not spend money on trifles that are gone in a flash, and that policy must permeate every aspect of your life. That does not mean being a miser. When you are generous, you make way for more abundance to come into your life. Keep your money circulating and do not hoard for a rainy day.

Whatever you give, you get back ten times more. Giving is simpler than you think; even a smile is worth a million to the right person at the right moment. We all have a variety of skills and talents that can contribute to others' well-being. Feeling scarcity is very depressing and keeps you down and keeps prosperity prospects down as well. You must increase that energy level and one way is to give. When you are kind, considerate and helpful towards others with your resources, it reminds you of your oneness with all of life. Giving also convinces your subconscious that you already have more than you need. You are prosperous and expect to continue to be so. When you give, you benefit. Thank others for the opportunity to give, because it makes you feel so good.

> Save and invest money to ensure comfort in your old age

After you have saved enough cash to tide you over for at least four months of unemployment, put it into a savings bank or money market fund, but it must be where it can be converted easily into cash. What is a money market fund? It is a fund in which your money is pooled with other people's and invested for you by professional managers in treasury bills, commercial paper, bank certificates or deposit and the like. The kind you want is one that offers security but can be cashed in at any time without penalty or loss of principal. A reputable financial advisor will help you select one.

After you have that amount stacked away for emergencies, you must invest the next amount of money you manage to save. Study the choices of places to put your money. These are some possibilities: savings bank (but with interest rates not very good), stocks, bonds and certificates of deposit, unit trusts, futures, gold.

You must also learn to move your money around. Time was when you could just leave money in a savings bank or 'blue chip' stock (IBM or General Motors or the Bank stocks; 'widows and orphans' stocks they were called because they were safe) and let it nest comfortably there and grow. If you do that now, it not only does not necessarily grow at a rate to keep up with inflation, but in some cases it can even disappear (companies do go bankrupt). Money can always make money, but you must check continually what is happening in the market place and not get trapped.

New possibilities keep opening up. Internationally managed bond funds are a good source of income. You have preservation of capital and a good yield with no risk. This means instead of receiving very little or no interest in the bank you can put your money into bonds with no risk and receive an income. Ask your financial advisor to help you ascertain your objectives and advise what is best for you.

The best way to make more is to buy value. Your financial advisor should clarify if you want to make money (buy value) or to have fun (speculate). Do not follow the herd – when everyone else is are buying, you should sell. When they are selling, buy.

Buy shares and unit trusts when they are cheap and hold them until the underlying values emerge. Each stock and unit trust has its own personality and your advisor should know which markets are best to invest in and most important when to invest. It's easy to buy, but your advisor's job is to tell you when to sell. There are bulls, bears and greedy pigs and greedy pigs always get their fingers burnt.

Read the financial pages. When the market is bearish it is time to buy. Cash traders are generally right and institutions are generally right.

All this may have changed around by the time you read this so check with your financial advisor, but not your beau. Men (and women friends), and especially lovers, usually tend to give bad financial advice. Better to seek impersonal advisors and keep checking.

Basically, it boils down to high risk/high return and low risk/low return. The more you are willing to risk, the more profit you can make, but you must be prepared to lose it also. You cannot afford the high risk investments with only small quantities of money in the bank and good brokers should ascertain your objectives and know how much you can afford to risk before even taking you on as a client to trade futures, warrants or anything risky. It is their job to know you as a client and advise you of the risk involved; so take control of your money. Save and invest sensibly and you will be secure for the rest of your life.

That is all practical advice, but before you can be really prosperous you must allow prosperity to enter.

Turn poverty-thinking into prosperity thinking

Do you let yourself have abundance? Prosperity is feeling good about you. It is not only based on how much money you have, you may be poor in time; do you have all the time in the world to do things or is there never enough time? What do you let yourself have abundance in? Love, success, joy, comfort and good health or do you just allow yourself to have a little? The entire universe is available to you. Do you see beauty everywhere and surround yourself with it, or do you live in drab surroundings? You can live in one room and still surround yourself with abundance.

If you look at the quality of your lifestyle, you can see whether or not you believe in abundance. If things that have quality and creativity and are uplifting surround you, you believe in abundance. If you surround yourself in drab and ugly and dead things that have no uplifting energy and dress in clothes that are cheap, drab and shapeless, you do not. You cannot expect prosperity and abundance to come to you if you are surrounded by the symbols of lack, and if you dress in poor, ill-shaped clothes you will not attract prosperity. If you look like the back end of a bus, that is what you will attract to yourself. It is much better to surround yourself with a few good things than too many junky things. The mistake that most poverty-orientated people make is to buy lots of cheap and nasty things. It is much better to buy one good suit, than ten outfits from a discount store (or a back street alley) that have been made in the back streets of Hong Kong for five dollars each. They come apart the first time you wear them and look shoddy. It is better to buy one pair of good shoes that fit you well and feel good to walk in than ten pairs of cheap shoes that after the first time you wear them, buckle and go out of shape and you get blisters.

It is many times better to buy one item of real jewellery than twenty sets of fake jewellery that discolour. Real jewellery exudes prosperity, looks fantastic and has energy. All genuine gemstones have vibrational energies that uplift. Emeralds have healing power. All stones have various properties. Plastic has none, looks cheap, and does nothing for you. Good jewellery not only looks good, but you can always reset it, sell it when you want to upgrade or pass it on when you want something different. If you give your jewellery to your children you pass on your energy to them, a double gift.

It does not matter where you came from or your parents' beliefs. What you think and believe will create it for you. Just allow yourself to accept, and expect to receive unlimited amounts of money for yourself. If you do not have something

you want, it is because on some level you are not allowing it.
What you reap you sow. If you are mean and steal
from life, it will steal from you.

If you want to attract wealth that you do
not have at the moment, you will have to
adopt an attitude that says you are moving
up. Dress the part before you are there and
you will rise to that part. You do not have to
go out immediately and buy a Rolls Royce with
mink lining and hock yourself up to the eyeballs, but
begin to enjoy the quality things of life. You can go to the most
expensive hotel or resort and just sit there and watch people.
While they are having their champagne, you can make your one
cup of coffee last for four hours. Drink very slowly though!

Know that whatever you desire you can have. But be careful what you wish for because you will have it

When you surround yourself with excellence and quality,
you change the way you think about yourself and when you
appreciate and see beauty around you, your life becomes more
beautiful. As you surround yourself with beauty, you feel better
about yourself and you raise your energy. And as you start to
polish up your act this gives off an air of confidence that others
see, and then they begin to treat you with respect.

Like attracts like and if you think 'lack', that's what you will
get. What you concentrate on increases. If you concentrate on
'increasing lack' and negativity, they will increase. What you
send out comes back. What you believe you deserve, you get.
Lack is part of the past and any negative thoughts are poverty-
orientated. Money is energy and if you believe your income is
constantly increasing, it will. If your parents believed there was
never enough money, you probably have the same belief. You do
not have to believe that now. You are only dealing with thoughts
and thoughts can be changed. Stop criticizing yourself. Change
your thoughts and you change your reality. Tell yourself you do
not want to believe in poverty any more, you want to believe in
prosperity.

You can choose what you like to think as an adult. When we were children we accepted what teachers and parents told us, but now we have a choice. Do not accept and take advice from people whose life is not working well. If your life is working well, do not let others tell you what to do. Your parents' lives may be miserable, yet they will still try and tell you what to do with your life. Do not allow it. Only listen and mix with winners, people who have proved their success, not losers. The proof is in the pudding.

But how much money?

Money in itself will not bring happiness. It really does not matter how much money you have; it is how much at peace you find yourself. Love, peace and expressions of the heart are all there, everything else is an illusion. When you find peace in yourself, there will be peace in the world. Loving yourself pays enormous dividends.

People who have just the right amount of money for them, are probably the happiest. They are not worried about too many possessions; their possessions serve them. They do not spend time and energy that would be best spent creating their life's work to acquire or take care of material things. Having too much money requires time to take care of it. Not having enough money requires a lot of time and energy just to survive. It is important to have enough so you do not have to worry about the rent and food and your time and energy are available to do what you came here to do, without having to be a slave to money. If you have the courage to follow the risk of obtaining your dreams, life opens up and doors open for you magically. If you follow your bliss, you will have your bliss, whether you have money or not. If you follow your money, you may lose the money, and then you will not even have that. Many people take jobs in order to survive, and then they find in mid-life that the job does not mean a thing. Their sense of vitality of life has gone.

In a few words ■ ■ ■ ■ ■ ■ ■ ■ ■ ■ ■ ■ ■

Do not give money to help someone out. Giving money is not the answer, instead teach them to create it in their own consciousness. Do not give away from a feeling of guilt, you deserve to have it.

You can invest in people though. If you see someone with good energy, who has goals and dreams but no money, invest money and time to help them grow and prosper and the more they prosper, the more you do as well.

The wealth of this world, its joy and happiness, are all unlimited. You can have all you want. You need only create if for yourself. The life force that runs through your body and mind is the most powerful resource that you have. It can be expressed in the market place and sold for money and used for the good of the world.

■ ■

Money in itself will not necessarily make a person happy, but a prosperity-consciousness gives confidence, peace, contentment, joy and freedom from the fear of lack, in addition to a tangible supply. Money becomes a spiritual experience once you recognize that you, your source, is the boundless expression of the universe, and your supply is limitless. When you know you are related to the one mind, you attract all good things in overflowing abundance and continually experience the joy of prosperity.

You can be as rich as you think and allow yourself to be. Most of us are content to just get by, and if that is as far as your consciousness can expand, remember that is your choice. You can achieve total freedom of financial independence if you choose it and work to uplift your consciousness to accommodate that level of completeness.

If you do not feel abundant and whole, meditation and visualization will help tremendously. Visualize yourself as being whole and complete and know that you are abundant. Surrender all your needs, desires and fears to the presence or source within. See your cup as full and running over, with no holes, any emptiness, shortages or limitations. There is a fountain of love within you, which is endless and in infinite supply. This is the source, the cause, and the effect. The world reflects your consciousness and once you see yourself as you truly are, and embody that vision, you will move above lack and limitation. Let go of your old ways of thinking and see yourself as strong, vibrant, powerful, prosperous, useful, loving, passionate, beautiful, worthwhile and fulfilled.

Women and finance

We often give away our power to those we depend on or to those we feel are superior to us. We lose our decision-making power when we deny taking responsibility for ourselves. Many women want the freedom to make decisions but still to be provided for and protected. They must learn to take responsibility for their own lives and develop a greater sense of personal power within themselves.

When you take responsibility for your life, you acknowledge that you created those circumstances. The more responsibility you accept for the consequences of your actions, the more power you have. If you can say to yourself, 'I did it, so if I do not like the results, I can re-do or re-create it,' you are off to a good start. You either take responsibility for your life or you feel victimized by the world. You choose to play the victim or to take responsibility and determine whose power grows – yours or someone else's. If you choose to be a victim, you lose power. If you choose responsibility, you have the power to do something about the situation.

Men have controlled women for centuries by controlling the

In a few words ■ ■ ■ ■ ■ ■ ■ ■ ■ ■ ■ ■ ■ ■

You were born to be rich, not to live in poverty, limitation or lack. Replace ideas of lack with thoughts of abundance and spend more time thinking about what you want rather than what you do not have or do not want.

Your true self thinks only thoughts of abundance and never lack or limitation. These thoughts are pure energy and constitute a powerful force that radiates through your consciousness. This mind power has an unlimited supply, overflowing with prosperity and abundance, and goes into the physical world to become forms and experiences relating to your concept of abundance. Money is a symbol of the divine idea of supply and your consciousness becomes your supply. As you have within, so you manifest without.

■ ■

purse strings and women have played the victim by not taking responsibility for themselves. However, changing social and economic conditions have caused more women to think about being financially independent. The higher divorce rate and the growing number of career women commanding high salaries have contributed to this increased awareness. The role of women in the workplace has changed and there are a growing number of women who are alone. They are now learning to negotiate for themselves and create prosperity.

Many women cling to the myth that 'dependency creates protection' and leave their own financial planning until they find themselves divorced or widowed and many single women leave the planning until they are approaching retirement. I ran a financial advisory company and had to 'pick up the pieces' of women who had never even written a cheque and had not the faintest idea what assets they owned or, if their husband had left them, if they even had any. They have never taken responsibility for themselves and had gone from being taken care of by their father to being taken care of by their husband. If a husband dies, for example, and the wife doesn't know the first thing about the family finances' there is a lot of emotional strain to deal with, as well as the financial worry of where the money is and what to do with it, if there is any at all.

I never worried about money until, after 15 years of marriage, I was left without any. With two children to support, that was not a comfortable place to be in and I now realize I should have taken responsibility for my financial position and myself much earlier in life. I urge and encourage everyone, especially women to start taking responsibility for their own life and finances now. Do not give away the responsibility and power to someone else. If you look to someone else, place or condition for your supply of money, you shut down your own flow and limit yourself.

Chapter 13

All is energy, love and light

The physical universe is energy. Spiritual teachers and metaphysical teachers have known for centuries that our physical universe is not really composed of matter at all, but that its basic component, which the scientific world is beginning to discover, is energy. Physically we are all energy, everything within and around us is made up of energy, and we are all part of one great energy field, which is vibrating at different rates of speed from finer to denser.

We are all like radio transmitters picking up energy frequencies. If we are fine-tuned, we can pick up what is happening in the world and what is going to happen. Everyone has the potential to do it. Thought is a fine, light form of energy, which changes quickly. Matter is relatively dense and compact energy and slower to move and change. All forms of energy are interrelated and can affect one another. As you raise your consciousness and awareness, you are able to pick up more information on energy and events likely to happen.

Like energy attracts like. Thoughts and feelings have their own magnetic energy, which attract energy of a similar nature. You can see this at work when you receive a telephone call from someone you have just been thinking of, or happen to find a book, which has the information you need at that moment. To create something, you always create it first in a thought form. A thought or idea always comes before manifestation. If an artist has an inspiration, he then creates a painting. The idea is like a blueprint that creates an image of the form, which then magnetizes and guides the physical energy to flow into that form and then manifests on the physical plane.

> The more you can visualize yourself as being successful, the more successful you will be

When you hold an idea or thought in your mind, the energy will attract and create that form physically. If you constantly think scarcity, you will have scarcity. If you think you will get sick, then you will. If you see yourself as being successful, you will be. We all create ourselves out of our own thoughts of our own self-image. When you are negative and fearful, you will attract the people and situations you are hoping to avoid. If you are positive in your attitude and expect happiness, prosperity and joy, then you will attract and create people and events, which will conform to your positive expectations. The more that you can visualize positive events and see yourself as being successful, so you will be.

Be conscious of energy around you and surround yourself with uplifting people. Dispose of people who drag down your energy. It is your choice to be with them or not. By doing this the good things in your life will vibrate faster and faster.

Using visualization to increase your psychic energy

◎ Find a place where you will not be disturbed for 20 minutes. Sit down and relax, breathe normally.

◎ See in your mind's eye your heart covered in pink, brilliant light.

◎ Count to nine, breathing normally but continue to see the pink light. Now move the pink light to the top of your head and hold it there for a count of 15. See the pink light above and inside your head. Visualize the pink cloud growing larger so that it now envelops your entire body, just as if you were sitting in an egg-shaped pink cloud. Hold this image while you count to 12.

◎ Next imagine a brilliant blue light coming from your throat. Count to nine and then transfer it to the top of your head and see it radiating as it hovers immediately over your head. When you reach 15, see the blue light begin to grow larger. See it expand until it is all around you and you are completely bathed in a shining blue cloud. Hold this picture and count to 12.

◎ Visualize a gold light radiating out of your forehead from a point between the eyebrows. Count to nine and transfer the brilliant gold light to the top of your head and count to 15. At the count of 15, see the light expand until it becomes a great liquid gold cloud that completely envelops you. Hold this picture for 12 counts.

◎ Sit quietly and drink in the energies as they flow into your being. Visualize vast streams of pure gold radiance streaming into your being from above. Feel the love for this energy and realize it as it tingles through you.

• •

Setting yourself free

The financial, political and social structures that are imposed on us today were designed thousands of years ago. They were designed to influence and control people so they could be manipulated into supporting the system, and to take away individual power. Most organizations and big companies try to tell you that you could not do it on your own, that you need their support and strength as an umbrella. I used to believe this, until I established my own business and found that not only did I not need the umbrella, but also I did much better on my own anyway.

When you let go of the beliefs and any dragging energy of others, you set yourself free. Life was never meant to be a struggle, yet everything is designed to control and limit through rules and regulations, dos and don'ts. When you can love, not judge, and are able to give total forgiveness and compassion, you are free and can allow truth and energy to come in. You can transcend struggle, restriction and manipulation once you have learnt the lessons and go beyond them.

There is nothing you cannot change once you have accepted total responsibility for your life. Everything that has happened in your life has been for a reason; a reason to grow, to expand and to overcome your struggle. Problems are good, for the more problems you work through, the more powerful you become, until you can combat any fear. When you face fear, it disappears. What you resist, persists. Everything that has happened to you is a part of who you are and was created by you, not by some force outside you. You are in charge and when you fully realize this, you gain complete control of your life. There are no accidents, only energy. When you can accept God as an energy source and concentrate on the godliness within you and accept yourself as perfect, you become more of the divine energy within. If you see yourself as separate from God or the God-energy force, you think you are worthless, life is a struggle and you are a victim of events.

The subconscious mind records everything, feelings, thoughts, and everything that was taught to us by parents and teachers and the church. They did the best they could, but most came from a survival consciousness of weakness and negativity. As a result guilt and the fear of sinning control us. We learnt from them that life was out of our control and would be a struggle. Beliefs were passed down from generation to generation. But now it is up to you whether you buy into the old beliefs or take responsibility for yourself and control your own life so that the lives of your children will be better.

These beliefs are your reality, your truth, and your mind holds on to them. If you look where these beliefs came from, you will find most of them have no foundation and are holding you back instead of serving you. It is only energy that has been handed down and you have accepted it.

You can overcome almost any negative energy pattern if you are prepared to give time and be determined. Your mind is strong and it has been thinking in old beliefs for a long time, so it does take some time to form new beliefs. Uncomfortable feelings and events are usually stuffed down with alcohol, drugs or food. When you have the courage to face these emotions and let them go, your energy increases. As you work with this energy, you will find people will want to be with you, they will feel your heightened energy. Paths will open for you and everything will seem to be much easier. You aren't wading through the mud any more, you are flying faster and faster and good things are happening more and more.

Transform the old, dragging energy to positive energy and see your life change to one of happiness, prosperity and beauty. Be conscious of your energy at all times. When your energy drops, your mind cannot cope very well and you will find yourself being argumentative and angry; things get out of control.

Taking charge

To be able to be in charge at all times it is necessary to spend time completely alone every day. This will help you detach from the emotional events and help you to balance yourself. People that make you get off balance should be avoided, but if you find yourself in a confrontation, walk away and try and detach from the person or event and bring yourself back into alignment. It is foolish to stay and fight; it is too draining. It is much better to maintain your composure, dignity and energy and walk away.

If you are in a relationship that drains your energy, fix it or leave. If money is stopping you, then have the courage to earn your own. If someone wants something from you, give it to him or her. By letting go or giving, your energy is fluid and it allows room for more to come in. Keeping the balance with yourself, and going with the flow, allows the energy to work for you.

When you meditate or walk in silence every day, you release the tension and revitalize yourself. When you centre your mind and visualize your day flowing, your energy clears the way so you will have a day that is smooth and free from disaster. When you start your day like this, you establish an energy that cannot be overwhelmed by the negativity of others. Unpleasant people and situations will fade away from your life.

Balance your life in the company you keep, what you eat, the places you go and what you wear. Be conscious of what you have surrounding you in your house. Is it uplifting or dragging? Is the music you listen to uplifting? Classical is, but if you listen to rock music all the time you will find it hard to stay balanced.

When you are balanced, people and events will not worry you. You can remain detached and in your own energy field, apart from them. The world's problems will not bring you down, because by being detached you can allow other people to grow, to make their own mistakes for their own growth, and you do not have to judge them or change them. By totally accepting them and yourself, you free yourself and speed up your own progress.

War, nuclear bombs, famine, negativity and stock market crashes are all part of life. Do not try to change the world. Start with yourself. By changing yourself, others will be drawn to you and what you are, and will then start changing themselves. When you can and do give, you give them the opportunity to give as well.

In a few words ■■■■■■■■■■■■■

Meditating twice a day will give you balance;
meditation for ten hours a day makes you unbalanced.

To go off and sit on a rock or be a hermit in a cave in
India for the rest of your life is not coping with life, it is
copping out of life.

Your experience of life helps you evolve and makes
you grow; you are here to experience life, not to escape
from it.

Energy must be delicately balanced, and as your energy
rises, your perceptions grow.

■■■■■■■■■■■■■■■■■■■■■■■■■■

Follow your truth and your intuition

Your intuition, or that little voice inside of you that tells you what
to do, is not a voice from heaven or hell. It is an inner communication that is moving at a vibrancy far greater than you are used
to. As you meditate and your energy rises, you begin to see, hear
and feel that intuition more strongly. Follow your own intuition.

I learnt the hard way. In 1987, a week before the stock
market crashed, I heard a voice telling me to sell. I phoned
brokers, money management people, and they all said the
markets were still going up, why sell now? The day before the
market crashed I heard the voice screaming at me to sell. I sold
all my clients' shares, but did not sell for myself! A lesson well
learned and now I follow my intuition 100 percent!

Most people think there is so much mystery in spirituality,
but after delving into metaphysical, new age and other various
spiritual teachings, I have learnt techniques that have helped me,
but I have also seen many people go overboard and try to
convert the world. If you can take the good out of it and remain
stable, and not go completely whacko, then there are many

advantages. Having a psychic reading can be very revealing, but do not take to heart everything that is told to you. If good old Aunt Maude appears and tells you how to run your life, tell her to push off! Aunt Maude is just as silly now as she ever was. Just because she is dead, it does not mean that she knows all the answers. She still carries the beliefs she had on earth and is still as thick as two short planks!

I have had some very valuable information from my father though. He died in 1984 and although I felt him around me, I just didn't want to know. I did not delve into things like that! But a woman friend of mine, who had a psychic reading in London, returned and was quite upset. She had paid a lot of money, only to have most of her reading about me! My father had come through and said he HAD to talk to me, and he could not move on until he did. Eventually I had a psychic reading too, and he did have quite a few issues to clear with me as well as certain things he wanted to tell my mother and brothers. The most exceptional event was just recently. He told me that my son in Australia was having some problems and needed my help. For some months, I had felt this, and I kept phoning my son, who told me that everything was fine, and not to worry about him. When my father told me to go to him, I went immediately and discovered that he was in trouble and that evening he also had a motorbike accident. Without my father's help, I would have been oblivious to what was happening to my son, so he was of tremendous assistance.

> Give of yourself unconditionally and you will contribute to others giving too

Most of these readings and channellings can be very uplifting, and if they help, great. But if, for example, you are told that you must leave your husband or wife, or you must give all your money to an organization, don't just blindly accept it. Do what feels right for you. You and only you know yourself better than anyone else. Follow your own intuition.

However, do remember that quite a lot of so-called spirituality avoids living in this life. A great deal of time is spent delving into past lives, instead of concentrating on this one. Use what makes sense, otherwise discard it! The teachings of most spiritual groups are very good; it becomes a problem when you become dependent on them. Many people do not want to take responsibility for their own lives, so give the responsibility to someone else. They think it is a lot easier. If you are experiencing emotional difficulties in your life, you are also very susceptible to unscrupulous people taking advantage of you. Just because they say they are spiritual does not mean they are. They may raise your self-esteem and self-image but if it is low and you grow to depend on them, you could become their victim. You can be persuaded to give all of your energy and money to them, no doubt for humane purposes, but it is wise to check exactly where the money is going and for what purpose. Do not believe everything that is told to you. There are many groups and institutions doing a great service to the world, but there are also charlatans. Each person is individual, and each has his or her own path to follow. What is right for you may not be right for someone else. Try everything, and follow what feels right for you.

Spiritual readings can sometimes be used as an escape from reality, but to use meditation and various tools for growth can be a big advantage in your everyday life. Do not go overboard. Keep your head out of the clouds and maintain a balance to your life. It is your creation, and you can contribute more by balancing and joining in with the rest of the world, raising your energy and the energy of others than going on a mission to 'save the world!' By giving unconditionally, you are contributing to others giving.

Cut loose and let go the tangle of emotions, habits and obligations to get the most satisfaction, joy, pleasure and high level of achievement out of your life and become the person you choose to be. The New Age Movement has brought to our attention useful information and courses, but many self-help courses are not really necessary. How about these: Creative Suffering, Moulding Your Child's Behaviour Through Guilt and Fear, Whine Your Way to Alienation, How to Overcome Self-Doubt Through Pretence and Ostentation, Guilt without Sex, Suicide and Your Health, The Joys of Hypochondria, Exorcism and Acne, The Underachievers Guide to Very Small Business Opportunities, to name but a few. In California you can even have your aura fluffed!

But many courses assume and make us feel there is something wrong with us which we have to perfect, fix and get right. Likewise, churches and some spiritual groups will tell you that 'suffering is spiritual'. So remember that being human is to love, the way human beings naturally feel about each other when not in the state of distress. It means being able to connect, to love unconditionally. It comes from inside; we cannot get it from outside.

Energy is a magic quality, which depends on many interrelated aspects of your life, mental, physical and emotional. Where there is energy, depression is absent. Loving creates energy. Negativity suppresses it. Being direct and honest with people about what you think and feel leads to greater vitality. It is possible to be both polite and truthful. Rest is a great energizer, so is meditation. Without them you will deplete your long-term vitality. We were all born with different energy levels. Some people have lots of vitality and others have a very low energy level. Love is the key to increasing energy. When you are doing something you love or are with someone you love, you tap energy resources better than at any other time. Your energy level is a good indicator on how much you love life and yourself.

Do the things you enjoy doing, and be with the people who are magic and fun. Eat foods you crave and live in environments that are luxurious and enriching. All this costs money and old fears about 'security' may come up. What if this or that would

In a few words ■■■■■■■■■■■■■

Live for the present, for the now, with energy and vitality, bliss and love.

Be fully who you are. You have become immersed in the programming you have been taught by your parents, culture and environment, but you can go beyond that conditioning and limitation.

When you accept your fullness, you are no longer adversely affected by situations or people that at one time created stress in your life. Let your spirit become free to acknowledge your true profession and work, and to become aware of capabilities you did not even know you had.

Release problems and realize they were created by you to avoid contact with your higher self. Remove all unnecessary work and interruptions from your life and free yourself so that the fullness of who you really are can flourish.

You can't get out of life alive, so you may as well enjoy it fully now!

■■■■■■■■■■■■■■■■■■■■■■■■

happen? Shouldn't I stay in my comfortable job to get my pension? If I spend all my money what will happen to me when I am old and can't work? I can't leave this miserable marriage because I'm too scared to provide for myself.

It's not easy to deny these fears, but a deciding factor could be: do you want to forfeit living a full life now, in fear of negative and vague possibilities about your future which may not even happen? In this way you are joining in with the fearful thinking game of society as a means of avoiding living responsibly in the present and risking to really live your life to the full today.

I have seen many people work in a job they did not like so they could collect their pension and live in the dream house they had planned. They saved and scrimped and lived frugally. The furniture was adequate, but they 'made do' until they had their dream house and then bought expensive furniture. But among several couples I knew, once they had been retired for a few months, one partner died and then the other. Their dream house was sold or left for their children. They didn't live their lives to their full potential or comfort and rarely enjoyed themselves. When you plan and save for tomorrow and not live for today, you miss out.

Chapter 14

The games we all play

We all create our own reality and I would like to share some of the 'games' I have seen people play. These are true incidents but some of the names and situations have been changed to protect people's privacy.

Case study 1: control through manipulation and guilt

He was a businessman and she a housewife, very glamorous and full of personality, but just a little bored with her very proper husband and their very proper and restricted life. She was beautiful and liked to be outrageous and outgoing, but her life seemed to be full of shoulds and shouldn'ts. Her husband would constantly reprimand her for saying the wrong things, dressing in clothes that were too bright and sexy, drinking too much, putting her elbows on the table, laughing too much and just for being herself and having a good time. 'It just wasn't proper and ladylike,' he would say.

She felt caged in, restricted and most of the time terribly unhappy, but managed to keep a mask-like face and pretend that everything was okay. She managed the household, the children and attended business dinners and functions without complaint. She was the 'perfect wife', but little by little felt her personality slipping away. She stopped laughing, withdrew into her shell and started to take Valium to keep from feeling depressed. She had no interests and stayed home most of the time. The more miserable she felt, the more Valium she took, until she finally had a nervous breakdown.

You might say she was a victim, but was she? She made her husband feel very guilty for causing her to be so unhappy and miserable and finally having a nervous breakdown. She controlled and manipulated him into believing that it was all his fault that she had suffered in this way and he had to be with her and give way to her every whim. She would often tell him how she had given up her life, career and country to be his wife and live in Paris, had had his children and as she was suffering, he would be made to suffer as well.

This scene went on for some years. To the outside world they appeared to be the average happily married couple, not obviously controlling and manipulating each other. Both of them regressed in their personal growth. The children were often told to go away and were quite starved of love. They were a nuisance rather than a joy. After all, 'children should be seen but not heard!'

Then she met the writer. He was a free spirit, childlike and full of fun and did not care for conformity in any way. He was completely spontaneous. He had many relationships and was attractive to women, especially as he was fun to be with and enjoyed life. He was married with children, but continued to have other relationships. He tried to please them all, but ended up hurting them because he could not take responsibility for his life and share a truthful and honest relationship with any one woman. He wanted them to love him, but when they did, he would run away from expectations. He wanted unconditional love, but as soon as he had a relationship with a woman, he found he was expected to cater to her demands. 'If you loved me you would do so and so,' she would say. He went along with their demands until he felt trapped and then bolted.

She and he, let us call them Mona and Thor, were attracted to each other immediately. She loved his free spirit and childlike qualities and immediately wanted to 'mother' him and do everything for him. 'Poor Thor,' she would say, 'he's such a child, I would like to help him.' He was a writer, but somehow managed to gamble, spend or lose money on the stock market. He was broke and she set about helping him. She loved his work and wanted to be his agent, not for money of course; she wanted to help him because she loved him. She persuaded her very proper husband to let him come and live with them because he cheered her up. She felt her husband's energy very draining and she felt miserable in his presence, but with Thor, she felt stimulated, excited and alive. His energy was uplifting and she loved to be with him. He made her feel attractive and she felt wonderful when he was around.

The household improved, the children were much happier and the husband was grateful not to be so harassed and was happy to have someone else take over some of the responsibilities of pleasing his demanding wife. Thor was indeed fun to have around. He was so relieved to have the pressure taken off him and see his wife happy, he turned a blind eye. He paid all the bills and Mona and Thor would take advantage of the comforts of home, car and the tennis club facilities that he provided. She discontinued her threats of suicide and

> Don't be a victim, take control of your life

started to enjoy life again. With Thor she could be herself, she could swear and laugh out loud. He loved her colourful clothes and loved to go dancing and drink champagne with her. Her husband was more than relieved to stay at home and let them go out together.

This continued for some time, then Mona persuaded her husband to invite all the publishers they knew to publish Thor's books. She wanted to promote him; she loved him and would make him famous. She arranged it lavishly. Everyone came and loved his work. She was thrilled and delighted and so excited with all the attention she was receiving. It was wonderful. Thor was delighted. He succeeded in getting a publisher and now wanted to enjoy himself. He had worked very hard and wanted to play, but not necessarily with Mona. He found her with him every moment. He could not move without her wanting to know where he was going, with whom, and what they were doing. He liked her but was beginning to feel very confined and restricted. He made secret phone calls and arranged secret meetings, but somehow she always knew where he was and if she was not sure, she would phone everyone she knew until she found him. One evening he came home late and she exploded and accused him of not appreciating everything she had done for him, he was taking advantage of her and she would not stand for it. She had worked so hard for him she said, and tried saying everything she could think of to make him feel guilty. It worked on her husband, so now she would use it to control and manipulate Thor. He was now her victim, and would have to do as she said.

Thor could not believe what was happening to him, but went along with playing the victim. She was taking Valium again and he did not want to be responsible if she took an overdose of tablets. Wherever Thor went, she insisted on going. She went to dinner parties with Thor as well as her husband. Thor was put in the seat of honour and treated like her toy boy and her husband was plonked at the end of the table. She made Thor's life easy, cooked all meals, and arranged his entertainment and clients. She gave all she could in order to receive his love and undivided attention. He was not allowed to move without her approval. She controlled his every move. When he had finished writing, she was waiting, he had to be her puppet to play to her tune, or all his privileges would be removed. She controlled him through manipulation and guilt and conditional love. Their love/hate relationship was built on her wanting love and his full attention in return for her generosity. She expected him to behave as she wanted him to and when he didn't she would make him feel guilty for not living up to her expectations. If Thor went away she would immediately get depressed, take more Valium and manipulate him into coming back. He felt guilty for leaving her like that and would return and tow the line for a while, until it was too claustrophobic and would then run away again.

They continued in this pattern for some time. But think how wonderful their lives would have been if they could have had a relationship without guilt. By feeling guilty it justifies the self-pity and you can use it to try and make someone else take responsibility for your life. When you have guilt, you get stuck and cannot make decisions or choices; it fosters the victim in you. 'Poor me,' Thor would say, 'I feel so guilty,' and, 'while I continue to feel guilty I do not have to take responsibility for my own life. I will try and get Mona to take responsibility for my life, my publishing, sales and my accommodation, and then blame and resent her when she tries to control me.' It is a way of being out of touch with yourself, and Thor developed guilt as a tool to make it easier for their relationship. It is a way of denying openness, intimacy and keeping relationships shallow and superficial. It is a way of avoiding self-esteem. 'If you loved me, you would do this for me; if you loved me, you would not do that.' Using love to control relationships is conditional love, which is based on limitations, qualifications, and reservations, unlike unconditional love, which is based on total acceptance of oneself and others. Conditional love is based on scarcity, on getting and giving to get, bargaining and trading. The identifying word is 'if'. If the other person gives us what we want and changes to satisfy our needs, we feel happy. If the other person does not give us what we want, we feel irritated and frustrated, which leads to anger and hatred.

What can be learnt from Mona and Thor's experience

These patterns start in childhood because often parents do not know any other way to be in control. They use guilt, anger and the withdrawal of love to dominate their children. When you feel strong and in charge of your life, you can come from the heart. When you feel lacking in control, you may feel you must manipulate and involve yourself in power struggles to get what you want. You may think you have to make excuses for your behaviour or tell white lies to protect other people's feelings. You are not loving yourself when you do this; you are giving your subconscious a message that who you are is not enough or acceptable to other people.

If you wish to be free, it is important not to manipulate other people either, but to give them their freedom. There is so much guilt in our lives. Connections between people come from the solar plexus, the power centre, from which people try to persuade, convince, control and manipulate each other. Loving the self means stepping outside this kind of relationship. To do so you need to let go of guilt? It is scary at first as you feel you have lost control if you turn over to other people, and especially your children, the right to do as they please with their lives. But you will create between you a whole new level of honesty and love that could not occur without your courage and willingness to release control.

You can learn to detach from your own emotions and the reactions of others if they take you out of a calm, clear centre. When you are willing to show others who you are, you open the door for them to expose their real selves as well. Judgement acts as an obstacle to self-love as every time you judge, you separate. When you criticize or form opinions about another person, you create a message that the world is a place where you had better act in certain ways if you want to be accepted and approved of. When you judge others, you set up a message that you are only going to accept yourself under certain conditions. This leads to self-criticism.

Your beliefs about this create your experience of it and it can happen in subtle ways. If you think people do not accept you as you are and that you must try hard to please them, then you will draw those kinds of people into your life. I believed this and found myself seeing friends with problems and when they were tired and non-giving and needed all my emotional support I took on their needs. At one stage my days were filled with other people's problems, so much so that I neglected my family and myself. When I finally realized that I was creating this, I changed my beliefs into creating friends that were warm and giving and exchanged energy on an equal basis. I noted friends who drained me every time I saw them, and the friends who uplifted me, and stopped seeing the draining ones. Loving myself more and accepting myself for who I was, meant looking after my time, my energy and doing and creating a good life for myself. My life's work was very important and I decided to devote my energy to that and not other people's problems. Of course I was there in times of need, but I learnt to detach and not get involved with them and take them on.

If you start identifying how you think the world works, that is how it will be working for you. If you think that life is a struggle and you must try hard for everything you achieve, then that will be so. If you want to experience a world that is caring and supports your image of self-love, look at what you are saying about the world to yourself. You will get what you expect and believe you will get.

When you let go of guilt, you will not be playing the same game as those around you and they will feel threatened at first. They want you to act in certain ways to fit into their patterns, so they try to gain power over you through guilt. I find myself falling into the old patterns still, but when I catch myself, I detach, look at the situation when I am meditating, and it becomes clear what I am doing and why I am creating this situation. It is a learning process and as I have changed, people around me have changed also. Through living my life this way, people around have seen that I cannot be manipulated and controlled through guilt, so they have stopped trying to do it. It was threatening to those who had used it in the past, and some friends I left behind. In my new way of creating my own happy reality, I did not need them in my life anyhow. It still fascinates me to see the games I can and did play and how it is so easy to get hooked into old patterns. By creating obstacles for ourselves we create growth and inner strength. Problems and obstacles are put in our way to enable us to move through them, to learn and to grow.

Case study 2: inability to change fear and hurt into forgiveness and love

Using visualization (see Chapter Eight), I transformed my hurt into forgiveness and love. Born in a small country town of Norseman in Western Australia, I went to live in the city when I was just 15. I went to secretarial college and then started working. I just loved the city; it had so much to offer. It was quite lonely at first, being separated from my parents, but I was very happy when I met Michael. I was shy and he was outgoing and sophisticated, and I was attracted to him immediately. He introduced me to the high life, wined and dined me and treated me very well. I adored him.

I was very much in love and very naive in my knowledge of men and sex. After we had been seeing each other for about six months, Michael invited me to spend the weekend with him and some of his friends on an island. They had rented a bungalow and after dinner and quite a lot of wine we ended up sleeping together. I was devastated to discover, a few months later, that I was pregnant. I was so afraid and did not know what to do; I was too scared to tell my parents, and certainly was in no position to financially support a baby. Michael was concerned, but did not want to be pushed into a position of marrying at such a young age and did not want the responsibility of a wife and child. His parents suggested an abortion and tried to persuade me to consider this option. I found myself in a position of feeling rejected; guilt for what I had done and what had been done to me. The fear of telling my parents and friends and fear of having an abortion was immense. I felt unloved and victimized by Michael and his parents. I blamed him for making me pregnant and Michael and his parents for forcing me to have an abortion. I felt so alone and was confused, depressed, desperate and unhappy, and did not know where to turn for help. It seemed like my whole world had come to an end before it had begun. What could I do? It was like a nightmare.

I felt very angry with myself for allowing this to happen; I loved Michael and desperately wanted the baby, but being so young was not prepared to accept the responsibility. After a very unhappy period, I agreed to have the abortion. As abortions were illegal at that time, I was very nervous and although Michael went with me, I was terrified and wondered if I would come through the experience alive.

The 'doctor' had some medical experience and I went through what seemed a never-ending period of labour. It was very painful, but finally a baby boy arrived. He was only four months old, but I could see his tiny lifeless body and grieved for the baby I would never be able to hold and care for. I felt part of me had been taken away; my dignity and trust in the world. I felt hurt and sad to have had to reject this part of myself. He was a fully formed human being who would never experience life. I had killed him and took on all of the guilt and anger at myself as well as resentment towards Michael and his parents. I felt burdened and ashamed for what I had done. I would never be the carefree, happy little girl again. I had grown up with a jolt and felt separate and alone in the world. I grieved for my loss and felt too ashamed to share my experience with anyone for fear of judgement against me.

I continued to see Michael for a short time, but when I was with him, I felt heavy and sad. His presence reminded me of my guilt, anger, and resentment towards him. Michael's parents persuaded him to go away to break the relationship. He went and although we wrote for a while, we drifted apart. I felt he and his parents would never respect me again and decided to have a fresh start and go travelling. I had tried dating other boys, but found it hard to have a serious relationship again. I did not fully trust men after my experience and wanted to forget it all by running away.

When I did finally marry and tried to forget about Michael, I still carried a grudge. It was not until 28 years later that I was able to forgive him and write to him and tell him my feelings towards him and the situation we had found ourselves in. I decided to let all my stored up anger, grief, blame and resentment go.

I had finally decided to take responsibility for my life and myself. I realized that I had created the situation and it was time to transform the hurt, disappointment and pain into forgiveness and love. Through visualization I revisited and relived the situation and saw us both as the children we were, and changed the energy of the situation from fear, rejection and guilt into forgiveness and love. I wished him well and was very happy to discover that he had his own children now and was married. Twenty-nine years later, Michael contacted me and we met very briefly. I was delighted to find that I really liked Michael and felt we could be very good friends.

What can be learnt from my experience

We live in different countries now, but that was a completion of our relationship and I felt very happy to have finally let go of all my poisonous and negative thoughts about him and our unhappy situation. I felt lighter and was glad that we could be platonic friends. I value his friendship and grew from the experience. When I saw him, all the old emotions and feelings came up, feelings I had suppressed and pushed down before. They all

---

Releasing people who have hurt you

To transmute disappointment and hurt of anyone who has done something to cause you pain, harm or created pain try this meditation.

◉ Close your eyes and see yourself pouring love into that person and then see he or she changing and recognizing their own spiritual truth. See him or her and you as beaming and loving creative beings, loving life and never having to reach out in pain.

◉ Feel the intensity of the situation with imagination and change it to love – it is as real as your thought form. Feel with total intensity and love. Change their energy by seeing them in a different light and you change their fear into love.

◉ In a relationship, see the other person as being happy and abundant, see yourselves laughing and loving but do not be attached to the relationship and what happens to it. Shift the negative energy by pouring love into the relationship but do not be attached to keeping it or letting it go. Complete non-attachment is the key.

◉ Be who you are and evolve.

surfaced and I felt sad but let go of the grief with tears and acknowledged the love we had shared together many years ago. Instead of keeping the old hurt alive, I faced the fear and then it disappeared.

Case study 3: shopaholics anonymous

Hooked on shopping? Michelle was one of the many, many men and women hooked on shopping. If she was feeling depressed, she would buy something and immediately feel better. It only lasted for a short time, however, and each time she desired bigger and better and more expensive clothes, jewellery and possessions. She never seemed to be fully satisfied and it scared her.

Susie had 98 pairs of shoes – all with matching handbags. If she liked one pair, she would buy it in every colour they had. Most pairs went unworn, but she HAD to have them.

Anna shopped at Christian Dior. She was feeling depressed because her husband had a mistress. The mistress had a credit card, with which she charged clothes and items up to her husband. Anna had just found out and wanted revenge. She made sure she spent more than the mistress on outrageous outfits. So outrageous for her middle-aged body that she never wore them in public. Designer clothing shops must make millions out of women's unhappiness.

Raymond had a Porsche in his garage, which he kept unused. Lionel had a pleasure craft with all the latest accessories, but it was rarely used because he was too busy making more money to buy the latest and the newest toys. The boat sat at the yacht club. Norman bought a shirt every time he went abroad and shoes every time he visited the US. He had suits made every time he visited Hong Kong.

Compulsive shoppers talk about clothes as rewards; they feel they deserve them. Some women trace shopping back to their childhood. Unhappy mothers dress their baby girls like dolls. Being dressed up can become an addiction. Susie felt so guilty every time she had a shopping binge, she had to hide her purchases from her husband. She bought things to cheer herself up.

Shopping addiction is usually hereditary. It is common when one or more parent liked to spend, or when one parent was very strict with money. Scrimping as a child causes rebellion and many get into credit card debt because of the need to buy. Men prop up their egos with car telephones and Porsches or Rolls Royces and women do it with designer labels to show the world that they are powerful and they have 'made it'. The guilt only adds to the pleasure.

Many laugh at their indulgences. For others, however, it can become a sickness that controls their entire lives. When the obsession causes the rest of your life to be dysfunctional, it is a problem. Going into debt, taking over the house with your purchases, making the family go without to support your habit, or to have relationships fall apart because of an inabilty to stop spending causes major problems in the lives of many. The common factor in all addicts seems to be lack of self-esteem. Most shopaholics have a low self-image and may have at some point in their lives had a problem with food addiction or being fat. Some shoppers buy things and take them back. It is the same as the compulsive eater who puts her fingers down her throat after eating, so she can keep her thin figure. It is her way of dealing with the guilt.

Credit cards are always near the limit and the chequebook overdrawn. It carries a thrill of living near the edge. There is a thrill in every purchase and the self-esteem is restored. Shopping is used as a replacement for sex and love, feeling inadequate, unappealing and not good enough. Expensive shops know only too well that to massage egos increases sales. Clothes are used as rewards and many women feel they deserve them. Ann hid all her carrier bags from her husband

and when he asked her if that was a new dress, she replied, 'It's last year's, you just don't remember it!' She filled her house with furniture and ornaments and when there was so much in it, she bought another house and filled it and then proceeded to buy again.

Shopping is a delight and most people I know love to shop. It becomes an addiction and an illness. I wondered why and came to the conclusion that those women, especially, felt unfulfilled and it filled in a gap. Their husbands worked very hard and were busy, and they felt unloved and neglected.

What I have learnt from these people's experiences

Before I developed self-esteem, I shopped until I dropped too, and never wore many of the clothes I had to have at the time. I was a victim, but when I developed my own self-esteem, respect and self-image, I no longer needed the 'props'. I loved and was loved by others for myself, not my image of success, not the props, designer labels, latest hairstyle or clothes and possessions. Now I am leading a more fulfilled life and am successful in my profession and my home life, I no longer need to show the world and prove that I have made it. I know it and am comfortable with myself the way I am and realize that I do not need the approval of others, I only need the approval of myself. I like to wear good clothes and wear beautiful jewellery, but no longer have the need to possess everything I see.

Like attracts like

I noticed a pattern that I bought things to make myself feel good when I felt unhappy or deprived in any way. I visited an ashram in India where there was discipline; no alcohol, no sex and you worked in menial jobs such as washing dishes for hours on end. I felt deprived and frustrated and, in a village where there was very little, I managed to find a shop that sold silk carpets and bought 12 to make myself feel better. Recognizing the pattern made me realize what I had always done to cover up my emotions of feeling miserable and deprived. Now I allow myself to feel those feelings, recognize them and let them go with love and do not have to rush out and buy something to cover up my 'poor little me' syndrome of self pity and the feeling that no one loves me. Meeting the guru was an incredible experience and there was an overpowering feeling of love in the ashram. The guru displayed an awesome inner power, razor-sharp intellect, prodigious memory, and diamond-hard strength of nerve. And she radiated joy, love and bliss.

With so many designer labels – Christian Dior, Missoni, Cerruti, Chanel – it is no wonder we forget who we really are. It is your choice whether to be a shopping-victim or not. Nobody is forcing you and the money spent on unused, useless articles could be used to feed many unfortunate people and used to uplift and educate people into a better way of life for the good of all. Self-respect comes from your power, not your weakness.

Case study 4: low self-esteem and the fear of abandonment

It is only too easy to acquire a poor image of yourself. Women especially are conditioned to believe they are inferior, not able to cope with life on their own. Life inevitably brings rejections with it. Winsome suffered her first when the man she fell in love with was killed at the age of 21. 'We had planned to marry. He was in love with me when he died, but somehow his death felt like a rejection. My mother dying added to my sense of desertion and abandonment. Then when a man I had loved and had been having an affair with for seven years opted for someone else, my self-esteem was very low indeed. Losing a job I had held, and worked hard at, for almost ten years did not help either.

'I found some comfort in joining a Tibetan Buddhist group

and practising meditation, but it was not until I started meditating while listening to Carmel Greenwood's tape, *Creating
The Powerful And Prosperous Person*, that I realized that misfor-
tune and rejection had given me a defeatist attitude to life.

'Everything she says on the tape is true. We are all wonderful people; we just have to look inside ourselves to realize
that. There is nothing we cannot cope with, because the human
being is a wonderfully complicated and immensely strong
instrument. To look inside oneself is to realize the greatness
and beauty of spirit that we can all reach by tapping our inner
resources.

'This has not only given me help in my own life; it has
enabled me to help others. To a woman, heart-stricken because
her husband had deserted her, I said, with conviction, "You
will come through this, because you are a wonderful person."
And I meant it.'

What can be learnt from Winsome's experience

Not only Winsome, but also most people I know, suffer from low
self-esteem and a fear of abandonment. This fear usually comes
from the conditional love of parents who manipulate children
into doing as they say by threatening that if they do not do
as they are told they will be left to fend for themselves. This
causes a child to fear being left to cope alone and he or she then
feels incomplete.

Most women have a fear of abandonment and feel they
must have a husband or a male in their lives. They feel they
could not survive without the father figure. When you love and
accept yourself for what you are, and take responsibility for your
own life, you realize it is very nice to have a partner, but you can
survive without one. You only need the love and approval of
yourself. It comes from you; you do not have to 'GET' it from
anyone else.

This frees you to be you and from the stress of trying to gain approval constantly from a husband, lover or boss. You do not have to please people all the time. You learn to take care of yourself first, and when you let go you find that others are instantly attracted to you. You are a magnet to them, because you have something they have not got. You exude confidence when you approve of yourself and do not need the approval of others. You do not want anything from anyone. You do not have to get love and approval out there, you know you have it in here.

Case study 5: fear of losing your husband/ wife

Doris was a middle-aged woman. She was a housewife and had raised three children. There was not very much money in the early days, but now her husband had risen to be the managing director of a very successful company and there was much more money, but Doris continued to think in her 'poverty' way of thinking and saved every penny. She scrimped on housekeeping and on herself, never treating herself to a good haircut or spending very much money on clothes. She would proudly exhibit her bargains. By not spending too much money, she thought she was being a good wife.

The problem was that she had not grown with her husband. He wanted a wife he could be proud of, someone he could present at a business dinner, who not only looked smart, but also could keep up with the business conversation. She would visit him in the office wearing flip-flop rubber thongs, her legs hairy and her hair straggly and uncared for. Her cheap dress would hang limply around her. Her husband, who had loved her very much, could not help comparing how she looked alongside his receptionist and secretaries, who were not earning a great deal of money but who always looked well-dressed and elegant with shiny hair.

But still, this was his wife and the mother of his children.

He tried to ignore how she looked and wanted to include her in his life. He invited her to business functions, but she felt left out and did not feel comfortable discussing business, so she declined. She would rather stay at home with the children. She did not like the summer in Hong Kong, so she went to England for three months each year and left her husband here.

Charlie, her husband, readily agreed she should go. 'Poor old girl,' he would say, 'it is much too hot for you to stay here. Off you go.'

He felt a little lonely at first, but found his secretary jumped at the chance of accompanying him to business dinners. He loved having her there; she looked smart, was charming, and to boot, she thought he was fantastic. She looked at him with full admiration and anything he said was absolutely brilliant. She puffed up his feathers, and his ego. He was beginning to feel young again and appreciated. From business dinners to social dinners and eventually to bed, it all happened so quickly!

He was having a wonderful time and felt he had the best of both worlds, a wife and children, and a mistress on the side. He gave her gifts and proudly showed me a diamond ring he wanted to buy. He asked me if it was good value. I thought it was, but asked him who it was for. I could not imagine his wife wearing it. 'Is it for your mistress?' I asked gingerly. 'How did you know?' he said. It didn't take too much to work out. 'What have you bought your wife for Christmas, a Mixmaster?' 'How did you know?' He was genuinely amazed.

When Doris came back, I took her out for lunch and suggested she spend a little money on herself and start looking a little more presentable. And maybe, just maybe, she could start reading the newspaper to see what went on in the world. 'Why?' she said, 'I am happy the way I am.' What could I do? I had tried to tell her without giving his secret away. After all she wasn't my client; he was.

Two years later, Doris came to see me in a terrible state of
anxiety. 'Charlie wants a divorce,' she screamed. 'How could
he, after all I have done for him. I have been a good wife; I did
not spend very much money. I have been a good mother. What
am I to do? I have given all my best years to him, and he wants
to marry his secretary! What a creep! What will all
my friends think?'

She was devastated and wanted my
sympathy. I let her wail for a while and
asked her what she wanted to do about it?
Did she want him or not? 'Of course I want
him, but after he has done this to me, I am
leaving. I can never face my friends again.'

> Use
> meditation
> and visualization
> to attract what
> you desire
> into your life

I explained patiently, that I was sure his secretary would love her to leave and she could move in. If she
wanted to keep her husband she would have to polish up her
act and work on herself. Forget about blaming him, there was
fault on both sides. The secretary not only wanted him for his
body, but his money and also his passport. I told her she had
created this situation as well, by neglecting herself and her
husband. It did not pay to be a martyr. All the money she had
been saving had been spent on the secretary. She gasped, and
hated me for being so blunt and unsympathetic. She stormed
out!

A week later Doris came back. 'What can I do? He doesn't
love me any more.' I gave her my tapes and asked her to visualize herself and Charlie being very happy together; seeing
them as a family going on holiday together. I told her how to
transform the energy around from negative to positive. 'By
meditation and visualizing your happy family, you will create
it,' I said. I took her shopping and to the hairdressers. She
started to take an interest in herself and started to read the
newspapers. I told her not to moan or blame her husband in
any way.

I encouraged her to get a job and to take an interest in some hobby or activity. She was not very happy at first, but did what I said. She did not really believe it would work, but at least it was worth a try. I suggested she entertain Charlie's business friends at home. 'At least that is a way to have Charlie with you. You are still his legal wife at the moment. Let him see you being a charming hostess at his side.' 'How can I work and entertain as well?' she moaned! 'Get them catered for and send him the bill,' I suggested.

After a few months, she started not only looking better, but her whole attitude had changed. Charlie wondered what was happening, and started taking more of an interest in what she was doing. She seemed to be more interesting, and people wanted to hear what she had to say. He even went as far as to say that she must have a lover! He found that he wanted to be with her more.

'She is such a wonderful person,' he told me one day. 'She did not make me feel guilty at all. Why could I ever have imagined I wanted to leave such a fantastic person? It must have been the mid-life crisis! I love her and want to spend the rest of my life with her.' He fired his secretary, but not before Doris had demanded she return all the gifts that Charlie had given her. Doris is now wearing them and looks a million dollars. She has gained confidence, and is very happy. 'I do not know why I had ever thought of giving in and leaving Charlie,' she said. 'My life is so good, not only do I love Charlie, I have all the perks of my husband's job, my travel, and my family. Can't think why I would have considered letting his secretary have it all!'

What can be learnt from Doris's experience

Doris still meditates and visualizes and we still have a laugh at her situation, which could have been a disaster, but was saved with common sense and visualization. Instead of trying to force him to change, she changed herself and then found everything around her changed. When she was attractive and proud in herself, people, and especially Charlie, were attracted to her.

Case study 6: overcoming debts

'It never rains but pours' so the saying goes. It certainly poured for Sue – she had the Midas touch, only in reverse. The previous year Sue had started her business, but as expected it had been slow getting off the ground. Meanwhile, Sue had invested in properties and by the end of that year had no work and large financial commitments. She could not balance her cash flow and was feeling very depressed and negative. The more depressed she was, the more things went wrong and before she knew what was happening, Sue was spiralling down into a black hole of no return, or so it seemed.

In December, she attended my course in Creating your Own Reality. Sue obtained the tape and used it without fail every day. She said, 'I had visualized myself wearing a red jacket to meet clients. Within a month, my maid, who was also a very talented dressmaker, produced a red jacket she had made for me without my knowledge. Even the buttons were identical to those I had visualized!

'Meanwhile the taxman had given me a bill for the previous three years. I obtained a loan from the bank to pay it off, and immediately afterwards was told by the Tax Department that I owed them another large quantity of money. I went to see the tax officer to explain my case. Previously, I had visualized the dismissal of the claim by the tax officer. This was in fact what happened when I saw her.

'I could not quite believe what had happened and could not wait to tell Carmel the good news, but the two incidents had given me great confidence and I continued to visualize creatively. I managed to sell my properties in spite of the dull property climate, and jobs rolled in. I have not been short of money since. Nowadays I do not look back, only forward and every morning I start the day with a period of meditation and creative visualization.'

What can be learnt from Sue's experience

You can use visualization and meditation to increase your success and prosperity in business. When you meditate you become much clearer in your thoughts and everything goes smoother because you can maintain a calm balance when everything around seems to be in a mess.

Before you have an important meeting, if you visualize the outcome – and visualize it being successful – it will be. It will proceed exactly as you imagined it would be.

When I opened my financial advisory company, I used visualization and imagined the company to be very successful, to have lots of really nice clients giving me their money to invest, and seeing myself doing a good job for them. I visualized goals of how much money would be under management and kept a positive image of how it would prosper and grow. By maintaining a positive, successful image, and seeing the company as being successful, it is. If you have negative doubts, that is what you put out, and that, generally, is what happens to your business.

To start a business is to take a risk, to have faith in yourself and your ability. It is easy to play safe and stay in your comfort zone and not risk going out on a limb, but it is only when you leap out and announce your intent and put your money where your mouth is, that you will succeed. Where intention goes, energy flows! You create it all, so why not create a prosperous, successful, happy life for yourself.

Case study 7: creating your own reality

Hilary writes: 'I first met Carmel about six months ago. I noticed that there was a course on Creative Visualization, given

by her, on offer. Since my mentor, Mary, had expounded upon
the topic with me, and I had never followed it up, I was keenly
interested.

'Mary had given me a book on creative visualization, and I
started reading it and got to the point where it explained how
thoughts were energy and how energy was magnetic, and if
you exuded negative thoughts and vibrations, you would
attract negativity in return, or, as Carmel Greenwood puts it,
"YOU CREATE YOUR OWN REALITY." After that I read no
more. I thought "THAT IS IT! That is all I need to know – let's
go for it!"

'I had learned Transendental Meditation, but it had done
nothing for me. I personally found the whole thing a bit of a
hoot, especially the initiation ceremony. Yes, my breathing
calmed down and went shallow, but after having said the
Mantra you are to let your thoughts flow, and I found myself
thinking about my mortgage or my overdraft or things that
were consuming me with worry, things I could not alleviate.
TM works for many millions of people very effectively, but it is
highly individual, and it did not enamour me.

'I was even more keenly interested after the evening with
Carmel ended. What an amazing woman, what a poignant
story she tells! What a laugh she has! She hugged and kissed
me with such warmth as I left that I resolved to listen to her
tape. I really did not believe for one minute that Creative
Visualization could work so effectively, sometimes she says,
within days. Nevertheless, I tried it out and very much wished
for one particular thing and visualized it taking place.

'Within two weeks it had happened. Of course, I am not
going to say what it was – I am far too bashful – but believe
you me – two weeks ago, if you had said to me, "I will make
you odds of 100,000 to one that your wish will come true in a
fortnight," I would have taken it laughing hysterically. What
happened was more unlikely at the time than China saying

they did not want Hong Kong any more and were desperate to hand it back to the British!

'I had my "office review" a little while ago – I was criticized for being 'too happy' – get a load of that! When I told Carmel, we laughed and laughed. Exactly the same criticism had been levelled at her when she was in the banking industry. We realized that the industry is not for either of us – clearly too many unhappy people around!'

What can be learnt from Hilary's experience

There is so much we can do for ourselves, but make no mistake: it is up to each of us to make it happen. No one else can do it for you – that is why Hilary was stuck in her stagnating pool for so long, because she was waiting for someone, or something to take her out of it – it never dawned on her that she alone had the power. Once you make the decision when you sense the timing is right, everything will fall into place, you must be positive about it or there is no point in doing it in the first place.

Who on earth said 'happiness never lasts'? What a miserable person he/she must have been! If you find happiness within yourself, then it will last. We all seem to rely so much on others for our emotional stability – it is so unfair on them! You are the one occupying your mind and body, producing your own life force, blood, energy, thoughts, etc. Why on earth do you want to borrow someone else's brand of happiness when you possess the tools to customize your own, reliable and continuous flow? Other people can restrict their flow to you, so for heaven's sake, learn to rely on yourself! You are the only person you can trust to make your wishes and aspirations a reality and if you can put you inner house in order first, then you can give out more and consequently receive more in return. Remember – you reap what you sow.

You can make things happen far more easily than your old familiar negative-thinking patterns would have you believe.

Nothing is insurmountable. Hilary has proved that by changing her beliefs she made her life much happier and more successful.

Case study 8: letting go of grief, anger, hate and resentment

James grew up in a family of conditional love, full of dos and don'ts, shoulds and shouldn'ts. He was controlled through manipulation and guilt and taught not to feel. If he cried, he was told, 'Stop that crying, or I will give you something to cry about!' When he laughed, he was told, 'Get control of yourself!' A stiff upper lip was what was required. If he fell over and was in pain, he was told to, 'Get a hold of yourself, and don't be such a cry-baby. You are just like a baby girl. Boys don't cry!'

He was sent to boarding school at the age of seven. He felt lonely and afraid. He sometimes sobbed at night, but was told, 'Don't be such a cry baby – only babies cry, not big boys.' He learnt to control his emotions and keep them stuffed down. He dared not show his feelings of fear and loneliness. It just was not done; after all, he was a big boy now. The big boys teased him; the teachers controlled him into discipline and forced him to lose touch with his self-knowledge. Nature had given him a natural way to release his tension, fear, stress and pain, but this was knocked out of him at a very young age. Control was a survival mechanism.

He grew up this way and was appreciated when he did well at school, by maintaining good marks. He rarely received any appreciation if he was laughing and happy. That was irresponsible and childish. He had to conform and fit into the system of control. He was taught to be a gentleman. If he did what he was told, he was good; if he did not, he was bad and naughty. He liked school though, as he had the company of the other boys, and loved all the games and sport they played. He grew up into a very responsible, hard-working man, not taking much time off for play and fun, and keeping a stiff, upper lip and a lid on his emotions. 'Don't let the lid off, you might find a can of worms underneath!'

He met a lovely girl. She grew up in Australia, where she had animals and space around her. She would ride her bicycle for miles and miles. She would laugh and sing at the top of her voice, and had quite an uncontrolled and undisciplined childhood. Her parents were busy with their lives. They loved her and accepted her for what she was. They did not openly display their love by showing their affection, but she always felt secure that they loved her for her and not for their 'expectations' of her. They were happy for her to get by in school; she did not have to prove herself and achieve or aspire to any great standards. Her father was a little distant, but basically she considered herself as having a free, happy childhood. Her name was Claire.

When she met James, it was love at first sight. They say opposites attract, and that was what happened. She admired his gentlemanly strengths, his polished manners and his success in the business world. He admired her ability to laugh and her undisciplined lifestyle. She would try anything and did not really care what people thought of her. She was a free spirit and liked to enjoy life to the full. She readily showed her emotions and teased James. She would say, 'Come on Jamie, don't be so serious all the time. Let's go and play.'

They travelled a great deal and explored the world. She wanted to know all there was to know. She was not held back by money, her needs were few, and she would rather go on a trip and enjoy it, than amass assets. She had the right idea, somehow she knew that you cannot take assets with you, but you can take memories. She did not choose to go into a controlled office atmosphere, she chose to be a writer. She loved her work and loved to dress very casually. They had such a good time together and were so happy.

They made a great team, had many friends and spent

many happy years together. She made him feel lighter and less rigid. With her, it was okay to have fun and feel free. She was very daring, and said what she felt. He felt safe with her. They were a handsome and loving couple.

Disaster struck when Claire was suddenly killed in a terrible accident. Everyone was shocked; it was so unexpected. Poor James was devastated. He was in a state of shock, but tried to keep control of himself. The old patterns emerged and subconsciously he maintained his old survival mechanism of numbing himself and keeping a stiff upper lip. He found it hard to just let go and grieve and cry. Being out of control was not allowed. He could cope and show the world he could and would. It was very hard, though, to keep all the anger, hate and resentment at the world and life for allowing Claire to die like this. How unfair it was, but his mother had always said, 'Who said that life was fair!' – and it wasn't, was it? He carried on like the brave little soldier he had been all his life, with his emotions and feelings kept stuffed inside. His body was rigid; there was so much rage, anger and resentment to keep in. Must not let it out, it is wrong to feel anger, must stay in control.

He pretended that he was okay, but he found that a great deal of his past anger and resentments were coming to the surface. The first target was his mother. He blamed her in many ways for his unhappiness. He felt that she had never really liked Claire. All his life he never felt that she approved of and loved him. He felt he could never measure up to her rigid expectations. She was very strict and ruled over her children, demanding that things were done her way and her way only. To her there was only one way of doing things and she was a little like a 'horse with blinkers'. It was black or white, no grey in between. On the outside, she was a very domineering woman and you were 'expected' to conform to certain behaviour. If you did not, you were punished. She maintained a household of conditional love. If you conformed, she would love you; if you did not, she was disappointed and showed her disapproval openly. If you did anything wrong, you were made to feel guilty. This was a method of control and manipulation. She was not a bad woman, but this was the way she was raised, in a Victorian household. Her self-esteem was low, although to the outside world, she presented the image of a strong and forceful woman who demanded obedience. It worked when her children were small, but now her children had grown up, they resented her and her controls. They were still made to feel guilty for not visiting their parents. It was their duty after all, and if they didn't, she would be very disappointed. They fell into line, and did as they were expected to do. She was a martyr, controlled by her husband, and she in turn tried to control her children.

Face your fears and you will learn to overcome them

James, however, after being married to Claire for some time, did not fall for this line any more. He was confused. On the one hand all the old patterns of behaviour kept surfacing; all the old tapes played on how he should feel guilty. But on the other hand, he hated to be controlled and manipulated through guilt, and dug in his heels and refused to do it any more. He refused to talk to his mother. She had not even bothered to acknowledge Claire's death! He thought she disliked Claire and him! He held on to these resentments like grim death. They were his comfort and while he was blaming his mother, he did not have to face up to his own unhappiness and take responsibility for his own life. Whilst he clung on to hating his mother, he was safe. It was an old pattern. It was secure, it kept him from moving on and living the rest of his life. If he could blame her for everything, he did not have to do anything about his own life. It was his mother's entire fault. He rejected taking responsibility for himself because he confused it with blame. If he took responsibility, his mother would get off scot-free, without guilt. He could not let that happen. Blame was his judgement, anger at himself for feeling stuck. Whilst he was blaming his mother, he could play the victim. It was all her fault he was like he was. She should have done this; she should have done that. If it wasn't for 'her', he would be the most loveable, perfect person alive!

What he had not considered, was the type of life his mother had. She was criticized constantly as a child. Underneath the hard exterior, was a hurt little girl trying to act brave and in charge. James saw her as strong, hurtful, over-bearing, unfeeling and a bully. She acted this way to control, but underneath, she felt unloved, unhappy and totally confused as to why James should treat her like this. She had tried her very best to raise her children, and had given every-thing she could to them. How dare he treat her like this! How ungrateful. She would not bend and admit that maybe, just maybe, she had hurt James quite a lot when he was growing up. She had quite a way of sending poisonous darts, which pierced right through your heart. She laughed at his inadequa-cies, making a meal out of them. This was really to cover up her own inadequacies, but James did not know that. If he said anything, she would put him down constantly. 'Can't you take it?' she would say, with a sneer. His self-image was fragile.

James continued in this mode for some time, until he was told by a friend to 'move on'. Whether his mother was to blame or not, was irrelevant. 'Get on with your life now and forget about what happened before. It does not matter whose fault it was. Don't judge, learn from those experiences and move on. When you do, you will feel lighter and free. If you can accept your mother the way she is, you will be free. You will never change her, but you can change yourself, and accept her the way she is.'

James did not like being told this. He did not want to move on; it was safe and secure this way. He did not have to take responsibility for himself. He could wallow in self-pity. It felt good. After some time, though, he began to realize that maybe his friend had been trying to help him after all. Maybe he would give it a try. He went to see a counsellor, who worked with him to bring all of his hate, anger and resentments to the surface. He soon realized that when you faced these fears, they disappeared. It was not easy, but he persevered. He had deep tissue massages, which helped the grief and anger leave his body. He went into a float-tank twice a week. He felt lighter and lighter and was beginning to feel happier.

He disposed of Claire's belongings, which had been surrounding him. He realized he could never move on and have another relationship unless he cleared the way. By clearing out the old, he could make way for the new. It was very painful for him, but also very releasing. He started to take a new lease on life and actually enjoy dating again. It felt strange at first, and he felt a little guilty for enjoying the company of other women, but soon felt more comfortable and formed a new relationship, which finally led to marriage and children.

He often thinks of Claire, but realizes that Claire had to move on too. She had completed all she had to do here, and was actually very happy in her other dimension. We all have to evolve and move on. Getting stuck in anger, hate and resentment and grief keeps us from all the future experiences. By letting go, we can move on and up and enjoy the future.

Case study 9: the tale of the lonely Prince

This is Rory's story. Once upon a time there was a young Prince. He lived with his father and mother, his brother and two sisters in a faraway land. He was a special boy. He had been born about seven years ago in another part of this faraway land. He was the oldest of his brothers and sisters and took this responsibility very seriously, always inventing new

games for them all to play and amusing them when they were
bored. He loved swimming above all other things, and was
very good at it, because he had begun at such a young age. He
also loved animals and once had a pet duck which, to his
sorrow, was cooked one day by mistake, but that is another
story entirely.

One day the Prince and his family went away from the far
country on holiday. They stayed with the Prince's grandparents, who were his mother's father and mother. They were
very old and kind and had a marvellous house, full of interesting rooms and gardens and farm buildings and even a pond in
one of the fields. The Prince had great fun staying there. He
particularly loved going to the back pantry behind the kitchen,
where the milk was kept, and, taking the old cup without a
handle, scooping a cupful of cream from the top of the milk,
then drinking it down.

After they had all been staying with the grandparents for
some weeks, the Prince was told that he was going to be sent to
a Special Place, on his own, in a few days time. He did not fully
understand this, but gathered that it meant wearing all sorts of
different clothes since buying these seemed to be his mother's
main business for the next week or so, and of course he had to
try them all on. They were not very nice clothes, but he was
told that everybody else at the Special Place would be wearing
the same kind, so he accepted that he would have to also. This
was the first of many things he had to learn to accept and make
the most of.

One of the things about princes is that, because they are
especially important people, they often have to do things,
which they would not do at all, if they could choose for themselves. Sadly, princes often cannot choose for themselves and
must do things which more ordinary children do not have to
do, for all sorts of good but complicated reasons, which we will
not go into now. These are the times when grown-ups tell you,

'It is for your own good,' and you know that means doing something you are not going to like!

What the Prince now had to do was the most difficult thing he had ever had to do in his life. He had to go to a strange new house, with his mother and father, and then stay there while they went back to the far country. He felt alone and frightened. He did not know any one of the dozens of other children or grown-ups there except for one other boy who had come to this place at the same time. He had never been to a place with so many other boys, nor had he any idea of what was happening at the various times during the day whenever the bell rang. He did not know what to do at all, and since he had always been the one who knew when his brother and sisters did not, he also felt that he could not let people know that he was confused. This meant that he tried to learn (and managed amazingly well) by carefully watching what the others did, and then copying them.

This is a common problem for princes who have different kinds of lives from ordinary folk and yet are expected to know what to do wherever they find themselves.

The first weeks were a very painful time for the Prince. Every night he cried and cried because he felt so lonely and homesick. And it seemed that the crying made life even worse for him because the other boys had all learnt a very strange Unwritten Rule in the months that had passed since they arrived at this place. That Rule was 'You must hold back your feelings.' This meant that if anyone cried or was afraid or unhappy, the other boys would tease them until they stopped, and later on would call them names.

Now the Prince was a very brave boy, and also very strong, and at first he used his courage and his strength to follow the Unwritten Rule, so that the other boys would accept him. This was difficult to do, and made him feel all numb inside and as if a part of him was dying, but it did make life with the other boys rather easier.

Something was obviously wrong with obeying this Rule, however, and the Prince's 'bodymind' tried to tell him (and the grown-ups around him). The way it tried to let him know was that it would send him a dream every night which somehow told him it was okay to spend a penny right there and then, so he would. Unfortunately he was still in bed, so the bed became wet and cold, and all the other boys, as well as the matron could see what he had done in the morning. This meant that he was both punished by the matron (who did not understand what the Prince's 'bodymind' was trying to tell her) and teased by the other boys (who did not understand either). So the Prince felt even more lonely and sad, but he had to obey the Unwritten Rule (he did not know how to do anything else) and the whole cycle repeated itself.

> Pay attention to your 'body mind' and understand what it is telling you

Now one thing we today know about 'bodyminds' is that when something happens with the fluids in the body, it is trying to tell us about emotions, strong feelings. When these body fluids come out, even at times we do not want them to, then the 'bodymind' is trying to release the emotions for us, so that we can survive for the next day. Sadly, even though in its own way it is very clever, the 'bodymind' does not know much about things like matrons or cruel little boys, and it does not understand strange unnatural Rules like 'you must hold back your feelings.'

The poor Prince would have gone on in this miserable way for the rest of his life if a magical thing had not happened one day. He was lying in his bed in the dormitory, trying not to cry, but feeling very miserable and lonely, when a very Special Person started to talk to him. This Visitor was a grown-up who the Prince had never seen before, but yet looked strangely familiar. He was about the same age as Daddy, but more loving. He said that he came from the Prince's future life, and that he could not explain more at the moment, but in time the Prince would understand and would know who he was.

The Visitor said that nobody else could see him, and that the Prince would always be able to call for him whenever he needed help and support and love. He told the Prince he loved him very much and would always love him whatever he did or said. The Visitor told the Prince that the Prince was as important and close to him as the Prince's own heart and brain were to his 'bodymind'.

The Prince believed the Visitor and knew that he could trust him with his innermost thoughts and feelings. He discovered that he felt so loved and safe with the Visitor that he could explain what was happening to him and ask for help.

The Visitor did understand and said that he would give the Prince special gifts to help him to survive and grow strong and healthy. He told the Prince that not only did he understand the difficult, lonely, sad state that the Prince was in, but he also knew that the Prince was being as strong and brave as he knew how to be.

The Visitor told the Prince that there were some different ways of living that took even more courage than following the Unwritten Rule did. He knew the Prince was strong and brave enough to do them because they would mean that he would enjoy life more as a result, and would be able to join in with the other boys much better, as well as overcoming his present difficulties.

The first gift was a suggestion that the Prince could experiment with asking other people (boys and grown-ups) for help or for explanations, even if that sometimes felt a little foolish.

The Prince woke up and went about his daily business as usual, but remembered what the Visitor had said. The next time that one of the boys did something that the Prince thought did not really make sense, he asked the boy. At first the boy was amazed that anyone needed to ask such a question, then he understood that the Prince really did not know and started to explain. The Prince noticed that after this the boy seemed to notice when the Prince was unsure about something, and he would offer to explain or to help. He and the Prince eventually became good friends.

This happened with several other boys, and also with a couple of teachers. The Prince felt so much more confident in himself by now that he was able to understand when he asked another boy for an explanation and that boy just got angry and shouted at the Prince, then walked away. He realized that the boy himself probably did not understand, and was too embarrassed to admit it, just like the Prince would have been before he had received the first gift.

Some nights later the Prince felt sad again and called for the Visitor who came at once, gave him a long, warm hug, and said that it was time for the second special gift. This time he suggested that the Prince experiment with a different way of looking at life in this Strange Place. He should try to discover how many ways he could explore to enjoy himself, whatever was happening.

When the Prince woke up, he again remembered what the Visitor had told him, and went about his business as usual. The first thing that needed a different way of looking at was the Cold Bath, which he and all the other boys had to have every morning. Now, how many ways could he discover to enjoy this? At first he found it hard to believe that there was any way this horrible, cold, miserable bath routine could be actually enjoyable. After a little while, however, he came up with one idea (he really was a very creative Prince, and didn't I tell you how special and brave he was?). This was that he could pretend the water was too hot! As he got in he could enjoy the surprise when he found that it was not going to burn him after all.

This idea was such fun that he quickly had lots more ideas; one of them was to imagine that he was a whale, swimming in the cold seas in the Antarctic, to whom the temperature was absolutely normal, and who could enjoy the freshness and the floating sensation of lightness as he put his body and head under the water.

As you can imagine, after being able to see this nasty thing as enjoyable, all sorts of other things began to be enjoyable also, things which he could not have imagined having fun with before. In fact, he was so successful at enjoying himself that he had to be a little careful sometimes about showing how much fun he was having, because some teachers, in some situations, could think that he was making fun of them, and would not understand what he was doing. What he learnt to do was to keep the sense of fun and enjoyment inside (in these sensitive places and times), rather than letting a grin or a laugh come out. Of course, at other times he would let all his enjoyment show, but the rest of the time he just turned his bright energy inside himself. This gave him a sort of sunny glow that showed outside, and the Prince found that people really liked being with him, and seemed to feel good when he was in this state. Suddenly the Strange Place did not seem so strange after all, and began to have all sorts of possibilities he had never noticed before. After a while he found that he did not have to make an effort to see the enjoyable side of life, he just saw it that way naturally.

Let your fears go and come to know yourself better

The Prince's life was changing very much as a result of these two special gifts from the Visitor, but there were still times when the Prince felt lonely, when he missed his family, or when things were just too much for him and he needed to give up for a while. One night he called again for the Visitor, who came at once and immediately understood. As before he gave the Prince the long, warm cuddle, which he longed for, and then said that it was time for the third special gift.

This time the Visitor suggested that the Prince was now strong and confident enough to challenge the Unwritten Rule. The Visitor told him how obeying the Rule was harming him now, and how unnatural it was. He also told the Prince that people who obeyed the Unwritten Rule often suffered really nasty problems in their bodies when they were older, when their 'bodyminds' had tried all other ways of asking them to change, but had been ignored. He told the Prince that it was not only okay to cry occasionally, it was absolutely essential, just as it was essential to feel and express other feelings, rather than pretend that they were not there.

The Visitor then held the Prince in his strong, gentle arms and just helped him to let down his old defences against crying. He stroked him gently and put his warm hand on the Prince's throat, which was all choked up and would not let any sound out. As he did this, the Prince threw his arms around the Visitor's neck and sobbed and howled and screamed and cried. The tears streamed down his cheeks, and the sobs shuddered in his chest as his breathing deepened. He felt himself crying for all the times when he had held back in the past, for all the sad, lonely nights when he had felt so homesick.

He felt himself crying for his Mummy and his Daddy, and wanting them to be there to hug and comfort him. He suddenly felt really angry at them for leaving him in this strange, frightening, lonely place and he shouted and screamed at them at the top of his lungs, things he had never been able to actually say to them before. He felt himself wanting to kick and punch and bang with his feet and hands and head. The Visitor understood immediately and let the Prince hammer his little fists and head into the Visitor's body. He encouraged him to kick the mattress on the bed and to punch his pillow as if it was his Mummy and Daddy.

After what felt like a long time, the Prince calmed down, and noticed that he felt really relaxed and at peace within himself. He felt really warm and comfortable in the Visitor's arms, and was able to just relax and enjoy the peace and love that flowed from the Visitor. Soon after that he slept, with a slight smile on his face, and woke up the next morning refreshed.

He remembered the Visitor's third special gift and the howling and screaming he had done in the night. He looked around a little anxiously to discover whether any of the other boys in the dormitory knew what had happened, but then he realized that the Visitor had used a little special magic to keep them asleep while this important time of healing happened. He knew also that he now felt free to show his feelings, and that, as long as he did not bottle them up, he would always be able express them when the time was right, and they would never again be as overwhelming as the previous night.

Because he was now able to notice what he was feeling, he was able to discover all sorts of new things about himself. He discovered that, for example, once he could recognize he was frightened he seemed to be better able to cope, even in difficult situations. He also discovered that, if he felt homesick and cried, the hurt did not last so long, he slept soundly and woke with a dry bed to face a new day with all sorts of possibilities for enjoyment.

By the time he had learnt to use all these gifts the Prince was nearly ready to go home to the far country for his first holiday. He discovered that he was really looking forward to seeing all his family again, and felt confident that all his discoveries would help them as well. He knew also that he need never feel alone again in his life, since he always had the Visitor who would come at once whenever he called, and who would always love and understand him, whatever things he did or said, who loved him just for being himself.

Chapter 15

Love, laughter and tears

When my five children were born it was such a joy to look into their eyes, into their souls and see such purity, love and joy, like a golden sunshine. We are all born with this, but little by little it gets covered up by hurts and rejection. I was told not to laugh too loud, not to shine or stand out, and to be like everyone else. Layer over layer covered the golden sunshine of love and joy. To survive I adapted and little by little my radiance ebbed away and withdrew.

I wanted it back and have been like a little bird pecking away trying to break through my hard shell of image, hurt, insecurity, acceptance and being unlovable. All of the fears were hard to face, but with courage and determination, love, laughter and tears I have faced, moved through and eventually melted them.

They still come up, but when they do I move through them more and more quickly, and remove them and let them go. I tried to sparkle from the outside by covering myself with jewels but when the real you emerges, no amount of jewels can radiate the inner beauty, love and joy that we all have.

Change is difficult as the people and friends you have around you don't want you to change and grow. It is like crabs in the basket. When one tries to grow, the others want to bring you down to stay with them, otherwise they feel threatened.

When you let go of your hurts and inhibitions and realize that your image or ego is not you, only something you have created, the struggle, survival and need to prove you are okay, leaves you, and peace, joy and love remain. When you come truly from the heart everyone knows and responds and wants to be with you or have part of you.

This book has helped me face and uncover many of my hurts and feelings. By sharing them with you, I hope you may regain the beautiful, loving and vibrant person that you truly are. I see love in everyone; we are all one, from the same source. It is only different circumstances that have forced us to do what we have done, and have made us appear who we are through our images and egos. Every one of us from the most egotistical man and successful woman to the beggar in the street wants to emerge, to shine and just be accepted for who they truly are.

I have moved through the hurt of my childhood and the anger of my first marriage to understanding, forgiveness, compassion and love. I acknowledge that from these experiences I have been given the gift of compassion, and have derived great strength and power from them. Whatever comes to me now I can deal with. I can laugh at the comedy I played, so serious at the time. I choose not to play those roles any more and although I share my life with certain people, I recognize we are all one. It is easy to love those who love you, but a challenge of strength and courage to love those who have harmed you. Unconditional love is what I want and I will only achieve it when I can honestly and truly give it.

Let the diamond of love and light inside you emerge and sparkle and spread love and joy and happiness to all. When you know and can feel the love and beauty inside you, you will have no need to abuse your body by excessive eating, drinking or drugs. There is no need to struggle when you know you are the source. God's intent is for abundance for all. He created perfection and you can create and maintain perfection also.

Love of the great self within and attention focused on truth, abundance, health, happiness or any other desire for right use, persistently held in your conscious thought and feeling will bring them into form. Where your thought is, you are, and what you think and meditate upon, you become.

I am very happy to have chosen my life the way it was

If you allow your mind to dwell upon thoughts of fear, guilt, hate, criticism, envy and condemnation and allow these feelings to generate within, you will have discord, failure and disaster in your mind, body and world. If you consistently think these thoughts, you will force them into your experience. Guarding feelings and thoughts is essential in maintaining balance in your mind, health, abundance and accomplishment. Discordant feeling produces disintegration, old age, illness and lack of memory.

To create your life the way you want it to be requires discipline and determined effort as most of our thoughts and feelings are uncontrolled. But the time and effort is well worth while

Meditation for inner strength

Keeping a feeling of peace, love and serenity and the continual outpouring of that feeling to every person and everything unconditionally, no matter whether you think they deserve it or not, is the magic key that unlocks the door and releases a tremendous inner strength, power and harmony. Use this meditation to still all outer activity of mind and body every morning and evening.

⊙ Imagine and feel your body surrounded in a dazzling gold light.

⊙ Feel the connection between you and your God within, focusing your attention on your heart centre and visualize it as a golden sun.

⊙ Acknowledge and accept the presence of the God energy within. Feel the 'Light' and its brilliance and intensify it in every cell of your body. You are the 'Light'. When you meditate on it, you will illuminate your mind, health and strength, and you will come into balance and harmony and succeed in manifesting for the good of all concerned.

In a few words ■■■■■■■■■■■■

What you think you are

You are

But

What you think

You are!

■■■■■■■■■■■■■■■■■■■■■■■■

About the Author

Carmel Greenwood was born in Australia and left on her eighteenth birthday to discover the world. After travelling to Europe she went to Hong Kong for two weeks' holiday and stayed 28 years. She started out as a secretary, then became a stockbroker and finally ran her own financial investment company. After learning all about making money and making enough of it, she developed her healing abilities, wrote books and produced a 'Go For Gold' series of healing videos and cassette tapes.

Carmel speaks regularly at schools and to young professional organizations as well as giving workshops around the world. She is also involved with Operation Smile (changing lives...one smile at a time) in Hong Kong and London. The proud mother of five children, she has been described in the press as `having an enormous, infectious guffaw that could coax the sun from the steeliest sky' and that she is someone who is `laughing her way to the top'.

Laughter and the ability not to take herself too seriously have enabled her to cope and survive difficult situations and survive triumphantly. For example, she watched her first marriage crumble in the face of her late ex-husband's chronic alcoholism. But she overcame this, marking her entry into the rank of world-class authors in 1991 with the completion of her book *Letting Go and Loving Life*. The latter explains how she transcended the experience of being a victim and moved to a place of personal power, creating a new reality for herself in joining the money-making business and starting her life afresh. Success and financial independence followed, only to have the life-shattering experience of her son, at twenty-one years, nearly dying from a drug overdose. Trying to cope with every mother's worst nightmare of dealing with her eldest daughter's and son's dependence on drugs resulted in mother and son penning *Wake Up Mum – Drugs Are Stealing Our Children*. This book is at once tender and gripping, but also a grim warning about a lifestyle that sees so many adolescents slip into the depths of heroin addiction. Mother and daughter are in the process of writing their story.

In 1993, Carmel and her family moved to San Francisco where she received a Certificate of Honor from the city's mayor, Willie Lewis Brown, Jr. 'for her work combatting drug problems in the community and improving the quality of life for children suffering from drug addictions.'

Carmel feels everyone has the ability to be happy and healthy. 'The only person that stands in your way is you. When you leave the past behind and live in the present you are free.' From living with the Aborigines in Australia as a child and experiencing their lifestyle she has been to Buckingham Palace with her husband to accept an award from the Queen. She now lives in London but feels equally at home in the USA, or indeed anywhere in the world. 'Home is where the heart is,' Carmel says, 'and I value every experience.'

Contact Carmel at:

website: www.carmelconcepts.com
email: carmelconcepts@ibm.net